THE EMBATTLED WILDERNESS

THE
EMBATTLED
WILDERNESS

The Natural and Human History of
ROBINSON FOREST
and the Fight for Its Future

Erik Reece and James J. Krupa

The University of Georgia Press
ATHENS

Published by the University of Georgia Press
Athens, Georgia 30602
www.ugapress.org
© 2013 by Erik Reece and James J. Krupa
All rights reserved

Designed by Erin Kirk New
Set in Adobe Garamond Pro
Printed and bound by Sheridan Books

Maps by XNR Productions
Frontispiece: John J. Cox, Songdog Photography

Printed in the United States of America

13 14 15 16 17 C 5 4 3 2 1

Library of Congress Control Number: 2013934088
ISBN-13: 978-0-8203-4123-1 (hardcover: alk: paper)
ISBN-10: 0-8203-4123-1 (hardcover: alk. paper)

A culture is no better than its woods.

W. H. AUDEN

Contents

Foreword

As that rare Kentuckian Guy Davenport, among others, has helped us to understand, nothing in existence is now worth as much as whatever theoretically might replace it. No place, no building or garden or park or farm or natural wonder, is any longer safe from destruction. This is because by the determination of industry and the connivance of our institutions, and with the tacit consent evidently of most people, every place or thing has become merely a property exactly equaled by its market price.

The inestimable service of this book, then, is to restore to a renowned and much-loved place its membership, both natural and human, and its history. Robinson Forest, like any place larger than an urban backyard, is a multiplicity of places, each distinct and even unique in character, inhabited by a multiplicity of creatures. The creatures in fact are too numerous to be counted, and their interdependences with one another and with their places are too complex to be fully understood or described. The history of the place is the history of rocks and water, of numberless generations of plants and animals, and finally of humans.

And so it is hardly surprising that *The Embattled Wilderness*, rightly named, is a collaboration of two authors who have collaborated in turn with many predecessors who have lived in, visited, studied, admired, and loved Robinson Forest. Their book certainly is not the last word on the forest. And we may hope that, because of their work and the continuing efforts of others determined to preserve the forest, they will not be among the last to know it.

As this book abundantly demonstrates, the study of Robinson Forest, like the study of any natural place, reveals it to be not merely a property but also a wonder. It is at present the property of the University of Kentucky, but as a wonder it belongs to us all. The long study of the forest and the records of it kept by university scholars are of inestimable value to the land and people of Kentucky, but so also is the diversity of its uses and interests to all who have been there, who go there now, and who may go there in the future.

The Embattled Wilderness, in addition to the instruction and gratification it will give to its readers, is exactly the full and discerning evaluation of the forest that the University of Kentucky should have authorized long ago as a part of its stewardship. That this book has no such authorization will surprise nobody, but that its authors teach there is at least somewhat to the university's credit.

Erik Reece and Jim Krupa have given us a book that we would not have had except for their intelligence, dedication, and generosity, a gift greatly needed and not at all to be taken for granted. It belongs honorably to a kinship of such books written over the last century and a half that have begged us for mercy toward our world, which—despite their pleas—has suffered ever increasingly as an accountable sum of exploitable properties.

One of those books, J. Russell Smith's *Tree Crops*, was published in 1929. Smith was "sometime professor" of industry at the University of Pennsylvania and later professor of economic geography at Columbia. The statement of his purpose in *Tree Crops* is a measure of our cultural decline over the last eighty-three years. It could not imaginably come now from any professor associated with industry or economics, or from most professors of any kind, but it exactly speaks for the work of Professors Krupa and Reece:

> . . . this book is written to persons of imagination who love trees and love their country, and to those who are interested in the problem of saving natural resources—the basis for civilization.

> *Wendell Berry*

Acknowledgments

We would first and foremost like to thank our editors at the University of Georgia Press: Regan Huff, Laura Sutton, Mindy Conner, and John Joerschke. For a multitude of other forms of support and assistance, our thanks go to Jin Auh at the Wylie Agency, Wendell Berry, John Cox, Phil Crowley, Steve Greb, Doug Mock, Rob Paratley, Randall Roorda, Rees Storm, Jeff Stringer, Melissa Young, all of the students in the Summer Environmental Writing Program, and the hundreds of students who have participated in the weekend field trips over the last twenty years.

Introduction

One of the oldest working fire towers in Kentucky stands atop a ridge in the middle of Robinson Forest. The view from the top of the fire tower is a study in stark contrasts: a contiguous fourteen-thousand-acre forest that is almost completely surrounded by strip mines. To look out over the forest's steep ridges—slopes that novelist James Still called "a river of earth"—is to understand that Robinson Forest is simultaneously one of the most biologically diverse landscapes in North America and one of the most threatened.

That is why we wrote this book.

Three elements—size, age, and diversity—make Robinson Forest one of the most unusual and important American landscapes east of the Mississippi River. In the 1930s, botanist Lucy Braun discovered that central Appalachia, with its eighty species of trees, was home to the most biologically diverse ecosystem in North America. She called it "mixed mesophytic"—not too hot or cold, not too wet or dry. Today, Robinson Forest remains a rare example of what many scientists have called "the rain forest of North America."

A century before Braun's discovery, the first white settlers began moving into these remote hollows. They were resourceful homesteaders who needed almost nothing from the world beyond the mountains. For the next hundred years they farmed, hunted, and ran their hogs up and down the steep slopes. Their lives changed very little until the twentieth century, when the railroad finally stretched its tentacles up into the narrow hollows. Timber barons were quick to follow. In 1912, Cincinnati business partners F. W. Mowbray and E. O. Robinson bought a thousand acres of land spanning Perry, Knot, and Breathitt Counties. Over the course of the next decade they logged almost every acre of that land. When they were through, there were no more hickory nuts left to fatten the hogs of the families who had settled this marginal land. The homesteaders quickly migrated to the mill towns that were growing up across the Southeast, and in 1923 Mowbray and Robinson deeded the wasted land to the University of Kentucky. The deed instructed UK to use what would become known as Robinson Forest for agricultural experimentation that would "tend to the betterment of the people of the mountain region of Kentucky." Such experiments were to include orchards, model farms, reforestation projects, and soil conservation. Ninety years later, Robinson Forest is once again a spectacular mixed mesophytic (though second-growth) woodland. Unfortunately, industrial development has churned under the mountains surrounding these fourteen thousand acres, turning Robinson Forest itself into an island of biological diversity surrounded by an ever-expanding desert.

From the top of the fire tower, one routinely hears the blasting that has toppled more than five hundred mountains throughout central Appalachia. Known as mountaintop removal, this form of strip mining is the world's fastest and most destructive method of extracting coal from the ground. Such expediency, combined with this country's thirst for cheap energy, has turned Robinson Forest into a bull's-eye on a coal operator's topo map. It has made Robinson Forest at once an exceptional refuge and an imperiled wilderness.

In an age of rising tuition and faltering support from state government, the University of Kentucky, like all land grant institutions, is under increasing pressure to find new sources of revenue. Coal industry spokespersons routinely call for UK to meet its financial obligations by mining Robinson Forest. Without doubt, coal worth hundreds of millions of dollars lies beneath the mountaintops. And because the value of coal is much easier to quantify than the value of mountain landscape, the argument to not mine Robinson Forest can be a hard case to make. But that is precisely what we do in the following pages. To make our argument, we must ask and answer two fundamental questions:

Why is Robinson Forest worth saving?
How should it be managed in the future?

As authors, one of us comes from the sciences and one from the humanities. We aim to answer our questions by bringing those two perspectives to these pages. We have organized the book into alternating chapters so readers can easily seek out the chapters about Robinson Forest's natural history and the chapters about its cultural and political history. Having said that, neither of us holds great respect for the modern university's disciplinary boundaries, and neither of us writes in any strict way within those boundaries. In the end, we believe that only an interdisciplinary approach can provide a comprehensive answer to our questions.

Erik is responsible for the odd-numbered chapters and Jim for the even-numbered ones. Chapter 1 is an overview and introduction to the human history of Robinson Forest. It follows the forest from the main entrance to the headwaters of Coles Fork, the cleanest stream in Kentucky, along the way recounting the early homesteading of the watersheds before they were called Robinson Forest. Then it tells the story of how loggers, strip miners, and the University of Kentucky all found their way into these woods. Chapter 3 explores the educational opportunities that the forest provides as a laboratory for experiential learning. Chapter 5 considers the management of Robinson Forest in the past, present, and future. It proposes steps the University of Kentucky can take to enact a more progressive management plan—a plan that might make Robinson one of America's premier research forests. Finally, Chapter 7 argues that Robinson Forest represents a crucial model for bringing our unsustainable human economy into line with the inescapable economy of nature.

Chapters 2, 4, and 6 cover the natural history and biodiversity of Robinson Forest from the ridgetops, down the slopes, to the streams that carved out the hollows. Chapter 2 focuses on the ridgetops accentuated by sandstone outcrops, sculptured monuments to events that occurred 300 million years ago. They are the remains of quartz sands that were carried west as the Appalachian Mountains were forming and eroding away. Chapter 4 examines the steep slopes of Robinson Forest and their flora and fauna. The height and steepness of the slopes create diverse conditions ranging from warm and dry near the ridgetops to cool and wet near the streams at the bottom. This range of conditions creates numerous niches, and the slopes thus have a greater diversity of life than any flat forest. Chapter 6 examines the ecology of the streams that flow through Robinson's hollows and are home to a diverse collection of plants, fish, amphibians, reptiles, birds, and mammals. Streams are emblematic of ecological resilience. Almost everything that nature and humanity inflict on the land above them ends up in the streams. Their ability to recover is remarkable, but ecological resilience has its limits. The one event from which the streams of the Cumberland Plateau cannot recover is mountaintop removal.

While we will argue that Robinson Forest is a place of exceptional beauty and biological diversity, its tale is not unique. The story of Robinson Forest is all too familiar to anyone who lives in the United States and cares about preserving natural places. It is as old as the debates between Thomas Jefferson and Alexander Hamilton about whether the United States should be an agrarian nation of small farms and small towns (as Jefferson wanted) or a country based on manufacturing, big cities, and concentrated wealth (as Hamilton desired). And because Hamilton's legacy so obviously won out, Jeffersonian Americans have been fighting to preserve rural landscapes ever since. We think of George Perkins Marsh in the Adirondacks, John Muir in Yosemite Valley, and Aldo Leopold in the sand counties of Wisconsin. But the struggle to restrain the forces of industrialization and commercialization continues today in every county in every state—anyplace someone sees an opportunity to convert the natural world into a stack of dollar bills. Those willing to wage the battle must, as Wendell Berry once said, accept heartbreak as a working condition. Certainly, advocates for the land lose far more often than we win. But the alternative is unacceptable: do nothing, let the heart harden, let the destroyers win without a fight. Robinson Forest is a microcosm of what the eastern broadleaf forest once was; but the political, cultural, and economic debates that always loom over the forest are also a microcosm of what happens whenever and wherever the forces of industrial capitalism come into a region that is rich in natural resources but poor by other standards. The story of Robinson Forest is the story of thousands of threatened landscapes, and we believe the lessons culled from this particular place can be applied to many others to show that the natural world is more than a "resource" meant for human consumption.

In the introduction to his classic story of the land, *Desert Solitaire*, Edward Abbey warned readers not to go looking for the western landscapes of his book, because "most of what I write about is already gone." Then he added: "This is not a travel guide but an elegy. A memorial. You're holding a tombstone in your hand." This book is not a tombstone; nor is it an elegy. Sections of Robinson Forest have been unwisely mined or logged, but at this writing the forest survives. We will make a case for its preservation by explaining its natural and human history, and giving readers a clear understanding of why that past is so important to ensuring that Robinson Forest has a future.

CHAPTER 1

The Cleanest Stream in Kentucky

Erik Reece

There is nothing more eloquent in Nature than a mountain stream.
—JOHN MUIR

On the first day of spring, I pull my truck off a narrow back road at the confluence of Buckhorn Creek and Clemons Fork, deep in the hills of eastern Kentucky. Each stream begins miles from here, up in the headwaters of Robinson Forest. Just up the road I can see the main entrance to the forest. This morning is cool, but the sun has just emerged above the steep eastern ridge behind me. I unroll an old topo map of Robinson Forest on the tailgate, anchor it with a cup of coffee, and try to get my bearings. Fading purple lines undulate out from the ridgetops, defining the contours down to each streambed. Robinson Forest, shaped like a horse's head looking east, sits atop the eastern section of the Cumberland Plateau between the North Fork and Middle Fork of the Kentucky River. The Cumberland Plateau itself is a 360-million-year-old tableland of sandstone and shale. Stretching from Alabama through Tennessee and across most of eastern Kentucky, it is the world's largest hardwood forested plateau. And I am standing in its last large forest.

The two main watersheds of Robinson Forest—Clemons Fork and Coles Fork, both about four thousand acres in size—drain into Buckhorn Creek, which flows west in a gentle loop toward Troublesome Creek, which then empties into the North Fork of the Kentucky. Most of the ridgetops in Robinson Forest crest at around twelve to fourteen hundred feet. A steep, straight ridgeline running north from where I am standing divides Clemons Fork's watershed from Coles Fork and Buckhorn Creek. The stream I'm most interested in today is Coles Fork. Stretching almost to the forest's eastern boundary, Coles Fork is the cleanest body of moving water in Kentucky, the benchmark by which the Environmental Protection Agency measures all other streams in the state. My aim today is to traverse Robinson Forest from west to east by following Buckhorn Creek to Coles Fork and then Coles Fork up to its headwaters. There, I have been told, I will find the remnants of a cabin that once belonged to a local sawyer. With one finger I trace my path up Coles Fork, past Panther Fork, Snag Ridge, and White Oak. Near the source of Coles Fork I read the barely legible words "Cabin Branch." That, I decide, must have been the site of the sawyer's home. I stow my map and start walking along an old logging road that follows the bank of Buckhorn Creek.

The stream is shallow, and its clear water moves swiftly through the low riffles. I would like to say that I am slowly entering a pastoral reverie. But I am not. There's too much trash littering the creek banks. Downstream, on Troublesome Creek, the situation is even worse. Recent flooding has festooned the banks with all manner of garbage. Half-deflated, muddy basketballs bob in the water beside a flotilla of plastic bottles. Plastic bags hang like ugly Christmas tinsel in the trees. The powerful flood currents wrapped large sections of metal roofing around the trunks of sycamores. It all reminds me of something Verna Mae Slone wrote to her grandchildren in a beautiful memoir called *What My Heart Wants to Tell*. Slone was raised just up the road from here in Caney. She was describing in careful detail the preindustrial economy of Appalachia, where a dead turtle's shell made a soap dish and her father wore trousers sewn from cloth her mother had woven from home-grown flax. "No Pampers hung from tree limbs along the creek," she said—a telling comment on how the economy of disposability has turned a resilient, self-sufficient culture into a disposable land and, as many would say today, a disposable people.

The farther I walk up Buckhorn Creek, however, the less trash I see. In a way, I am walking back into another time—a time when Slone and her family "lived, loved, fought and died undisturbed by the outside world, protected and imprisoned by its hills." And it's true, the steep slopes can feel imprisoning. Across the creek, the bank rises sharply, covered in thick rhododendron. The stream itself slowly navigates deadfalls and the silted dunes left behind by the floodwater.

I come to a spot where the current cuts a wide loop around a broad bottomland uncharacteristic of the narrow mountain valleys. Mayapple grows thickly near the stream bank, which the Buckhorn's shallow water has carved into rows of sandy scallops. Sycamores grow in the spongy mud. On the other side of the stream a vertical wall of sandstone rises thirty feet to a bench where the roots of hemlock cling to the rock face with what looks like human urgency. Down here in the clearing, known as Mart Bottom, the grass is high and untended.

Sometime between 1780 and 1797, a man named William Noble arrived in this very spot with his wife and several members of their extended families. Some say they migrated to this clearing through the Cumberland Gap, spending their first winter in rock shelters like the ones that overhang this bend of the Buckhorn. By other accounts, they followed the Licking River down from the north. Whatever the case, the Nobles and the Neaces were the first families of Scots-Irish descent to settle in what is now Breathitt County, Kentucky. Perhaps William Noble had fought in George Washington's Continental Army. In 1779 the state of Virginia established a land office that allowed Revolutionary War veterans to claim "waste and unappropriated lands" west of the Cumberland Mountains and south of the Ohio River—in other words, what is now eastern Kentucky. The Nobles and Neaces eventually intermarried with a French family, the Fugates, and the mailboxes you pass as you drive to Robinson Forest along Buckhorn and Troublesome Creeks still bear these three family names.

Only in the late 1820s did other white settlers begin to move into this area, the most remote part of the eastern coalfields. And it wasn't until 1835 that Kentucky counties were authorized to sell this unclaimed wilderness as Kentucky land warrants. The land was usually sold in fifty- or hundred-acre tracts, for $2.50 or $5 respectively, and the money was used to build roads and courthouses. By 1855, the year Walt Whitman published his first edition of *Leaves of Grass*, ten landowners had moved onto the Buckhorn. And certainly those homesteaders would have resembled the freedom-loving "roughs" Whitman celebrated in his epic poem. The first county warrants on Coles Fork and Clemons Fork were issued in 1848. Strangely, though, Benjamin Clemons, whose name the northern stream bears, actually claimed one hundred acres on Coles Fork, whereas a man named Wilson Barnett claimed the first one hundred acres on Clemons Fork.

An old photograph from the University of Kentucky archives, taken somewhere in Robinson Forest, shows what those clearings would have looked like before the timber barons arrived. A modest log cabin with wide chinking stands in the background, but a fenced garden—a "right smart"—fills most of the picture. There are neat rows of bunch beans, peas, cabbage, peppers, onions, cucumbers, turnips, and tobacco. The garden soil would have been amended with animal manure and wood ashes. The hillsides and bottomlands beyond the frame of this photo would have been planted with corn. Mountain farmers usually chose a northeast slope where trees had already been cut for firewood, then prepared the soil with a grub hoe. After a couple of years, when the root matter had decayed, the farmer would plow the hillside with a mule. Field beans would climb the cornstalks, and cushaw would grow in their shade. Some Native American tribes called this planting method the "three sisters," and Appalachian settlers clearly employed it as well. A farmer could expect a yield of about twenty bushels of corn per acre—by no means a bumper crop, but enough to feed the two gristmills that were soon built on Clemons Fork, on the other side of the ridge. When a heavy rain washed out the hillside, the farmer simply left it for another. Soil specialist Paul Kalisz told me that yellow poplars, redbud, and dogwood—which are "calcium pumps"—would have quickly reclaimed the abandoned hillsides. In fact, he said, the old fields actually improved the soil quality of these hillsides, at least by conventional standards. "As long as populations are low," Kalisz told me, "mountain agriculture is a viable system. You just grow it for a while, then let it go." Today, when you see a hillside on the Cumberland Plateau covered with yellow poplars, you are looking at what once was a modest mountain homestead.

Further still beyond the photo's frame there would have been milk cows and sheep, horses, and oxen. The family's hogs would have run loose in the woods, getting fat on hickory nuts and other mast. Verna Mae Slone remembered her father surveying his gardens and fields at sunset and saying, "This is the way Eden must have looked before sin entered the world." It is certainly what the cloistered world of these mountains looked like before the railroads arrived.

The Kentucky Union Railway, running from Lexington to Jackson, Kentucky, twenty-five miles west of Robinson Forest, was completed in 1890. Timber speculators followed, buying up large parcels throughout Breathitt and Knott Counties. Commercial loggers came in that same year, hiring local men to cut the timber and load it onto three-wheeled carts that ran along "tram roads," wooden rails covered with metal—sometimes iron—tracks. These operations never grew very large, but two timber companies in particular, Breathitt Coal, Iron and Lumber (bcil) and Taylor & Crate (T&C), engaged in a contentious and litigious struggle over tracts throughout what is now Robinson Forest. For two decades they fought each other in court and by proxy on the land itself.

In a 1914 talk to the Literary Club of Cincinnati, attorney Shelley Rouse delivered a spirited reflection on his experience trying to settle the disputes in "Bloody Breathitt." In the 1890s, bcil sent Rouse, then a junior litigator, into the fray, apparently on the suggestion of a senior partner's wife, who reasoned that Rouse "is young and unmarried and it won't make any difference about him." In his short memoir, called "Troubles on Troublesome," Rouse described what happened.

> Having no defense at that time, either to the charge of being unmarried or of being young, I was speedily convicted and without further ado, bade farewell to my friends, and two days afterward, having left the then new railroad at the point between Fincastle and Beattyville, I followed the windings of Devil's Creek back in the wild section over which at that time one Jed Spencer held full sway as the arbiter of men and fortunes as well as of "moonshine" stills. At that period the art of manufacturing liquor by the light of the moon was at its height and feud fighting was carried on in a dozen counties with all the primitive savagery of the Scottish Highlands;

each man was a law unto himself, and held his state through the loyalty of his individual clan and the power of his own good arm.

The mountaineers' "treatment of me was uniformly courteous," he admitted "and, their hospitality though poor, was generous." The main point of contention was which company held a legal claim to fifty-five hundred acres of what is now the northern section of Robinson Forest. "A great array of Counsel eminent and otherwise was engaged on either side," Rouse observed in a voice of bemused detachment that suggests the influence of Mark Twain and John Fox Jr. During one trial, the lead lawyer for BCIL invoked the biblical story of King Ahab and his wife, Jezebel, who allowed temples of Baal inside Israel, to accuse T&C of seizing timber with forged documents and impure motives. For outsiders to stake false claims in the Eden of eastern Kentucky was just such a heresy. It should be said that BCIL was owned by outsiders as well, but Rouse let that detail slide.

During another trial, a T&C lawyer tried to impugn the testimony of ninety-one-year-old John Hagins by calling into question the old man's memory. At issue was a piece of land called Peg Brown Branch, so named for a woman of dubious reputation who had lived on that tributary of Clemons Fork with a number of men and the children she bore them (Verna Mae Slone would have called Peg Brown a "ridge runner"). Rouse recorded the cross-examination of Hagins as follows:

Q: Uncle John, is your memory good?
A: Mostly, I recollect things away back yon better than things that happens now.
Q: Well, Uncle John, in them days they was lively times on Buckhorn and Troublesome, wasn't they?
A: Not much, not so much. The country was not much settled, and people didn't get real riled like until and during the [Civil] War, and since then the killins and gwi-ins on has been frequent.
Q: Well, Uncle John, tell us when Peg Brown moved on the Branch that afterwards was called by her name.
A: She moved thar in 1846.
Q: Mr. Hagins, can you read or write?
A: Well, only moderate.

Q: Now sir, will you tell the Commissioner, how it happens after a lapse of sixty-three years, that you definitely state the year in which the person you have named went to reside at that place you have described?

A: I don't really make out what you mean.

Q: Well, how do you remember that?

A: Oh, stranger, being that you are a "furriner," I'll tell you—it was this way—I was elected a constable in 1846 and that year Peg Brown came to the cabin, and when they were doing the first clearin' at the mouth of that creek right after the cabin were built, I went thar and arrested the man she had took up with, for hog stealin'. Don't you reckon that would make me recollect hit?

To that, Rouse only added, "And it certainly did, so far as any further cross examination was concerned."

Throughout the legal wrangling, Rouse remained perplexed by the highlander's "unwillingness to vouch for the integrity of his genealogy." For example, when Lawson Noble was asked about his relation to Ira Noble, one of the first men to settle land along Clemons Fork, Lawson replied, "Well, he was said to be my father." The lawyer pressed, "You are the son of Ira Noble?" Response: "Yes sir. Said to be." Presumably, if there were any undisclosed sins of the father, ones that a court could prosecute, the son didn't wish to be burdened with the information or the association. Ira Noble finally left Clemons Fork for the nearby town of Jackson when he grew tired of living, in Rouse's phrase, "so nigh the Rebel Path"—that is, the route through the mountains "by which the Kentuckians surreptitiously left the 'settlements' to join the Confederate armies in Virginia and North Carolina."

One of the watersheds where Ira Noble lived was called Little Mill-seat after the gristmill one of the Nobles had built there. In an attempt to stake a legal claim through squatter's rights to the area around Little Millseat, T&C hired a man named Babe Haddix to build a shanty there and plant some tobacco. Haddix's twelve-by-fourteen-foot cabin of unhewn logs became, Rouse noted, "the storm center about which the contending parties struggled for many months before the Courts were called upon to settle the controversy." BCIL hired a man named Green Noble, presumably a relative of Ira's, to pull up Haddix's tobacco and take possession of his cabin. Which he did in short order. Green Noble soon met his demise, though (Rouse alluded only to "the fortunes of war"), and Haddix repossessed the cabin and put in another garden. But shortly thereafter another Noble, Sylvester, cut his fences and, as Haddix told a judge, "hauled his plunder through." Haddix rebuilt the cabin, this time installing a man named Harry Lovings to live there in his stead.

At that point, BCIL tried to have the issue settled before a magistrate. But T&C convinced seventy-five men who lived next to Troublesome Creek to attend the hearing, carrying arms, and they created a decidedly charged air around the courthouse. Later, a lawyer cross-examined Henry Lovings as to whether he was armed during his own testimony:

Q: Did you have a gun?
A: Yes sir. Babe Haddix had given me a gun to squirrel hunt with.
Q: Babe was afraid the squirrels would devour you while the trial was going on was he?
A: I don't know—he just said for me to keep the gun close about to squirrel hunt with.

In the end, no verdict was reached, the gunmen departed peacefully, and in 1912 BCIL sold its claim to all land along Clemons Fork to T&C. Two days later, T&C transferred all of its holdings in Perry, Knot, and Breathitt Counties to the Mowbray and Robinson Company of Cincinnati.

At that point the tall timber really started to fall. Mowbray-Robinson immediately built a boardinghouse that accommodated about fifty men, hired Ellen Noble, a descendent of William Noble, to cook for them, and built her a cabin next to Clemons Fork. Mowbray-Robinson erected large sawmills twenty miles away in the town of Quicksand on the banks of the Kentucky River. There they dug storage ponds and pumped steam into them from the mills so the operation could run all year long. Houses, a commissary, and a clubhouse quickly followed.

Soon the Mowbray-Robinson operation was hauling out one hundred thousand board feet of timber a day. The company started along Clemons Fork and then, in 1919, purchased the entire Coles Fork watershed for sixty-one thousand dollars. Working for a dollar a day, men armed with crosscut saws felled giant trees six feet in diameter and eighty to one hundred feet tall. Then they hitched the logs to oxen or mules and snaked the timber down the hillsides. Using a tool called a cant hook or peavey, they maneuvered the logs to the bottomlands, where Mowbray-Robinson had laid a gauge line. A Shay locomotive hauled one load a day from Buckhorn to Quicksand, and more timber was moved along the Kentucky Union line that had been set down in 1890. The trains could easily haul out the massive oaks that had been too heavy for the earlier loggers to float downstream.

By 1922, the twenty-three square miles of timberland Mowbray-Robinson had purchased was nearly barren of trees. A few small hickories and hemlocks remained, but they didn't produce enough mast for the hogs to eat. Census records show a rapid decline in livestock husbandry throughout Breathitt County. The families that had settled along Buckhorn Creek a generation earlier disappeared. The men went to work for the commercial loggers, and the women went to work in mills. In his only book, *Notes on the State of Virginia*, Thomas Jefferson had urged American farmers not to succumb to the grind of the factory floor, but rather to remain "the chosen people of God, if ever he had a chosen people, whose breasts he made his peculiar deposit of substantial and genuine virtue." But almost overnight, it seems, Jefferson's dream of an agrarian countryside was displaced by Alexander Hamilton's dream of industrialism. Historian Ronald Eller reported that by 1930, three-quarters of a million mountaineers had abandoned their land and migrated to mill towns. Most women stopped spinning their own wool and flax and gathering their own honey. Those things would have to be purchased with the money they made in the mills. Eighty percent of the mill workers were women and children.

Mowbray and Robinson had no more use for the denuded land, and so in 1922 they formed the E. O. Robinson Mountain Fund, which a year later, on October 10, 1923, deeded the land in trust to the University of Kentucky. Robinson specified at the time that the land should be used for "practical demonstration of reforestation" to ensure "the betterment of the people of the mountain region of Kentucky." Almost ninety years later, that reforestation—conducted almost entirely and, one dares to say "practically," by the forest itself—has turned bald hillsides into the state's cleanest watersheds. The outcome was initially in doubt. In 1924 the Kentucky General Assembly passed an appropriations act that guaranteed the University of Kentucky twenty-five thousand dollars a year to establish and operate the Robinson Sub-experiment Station at Quicksand. The university hired C. H. Burrage as the first forester (owning a horse was a requirement for the job), and he set about establishing the boundaries of Robinson Forest and inventorying its trees. Meanwhile, UK had its hands full trying to evict squatters and loggers who had worked for Mowbray-Robinson. The university hired Tony Cheney of Ary, Kentucky, to tear down houses and sheds throughout the forest; he was paid with whatever materials he could salvage in the process. Understandably, the residents of the shanties resented their removal, especially during the harsh winter of 1923, and the history of arson in Robinson Forest began at that time. During 1925 and 1926 about two thousand acres of the forest burned. UK hired Jim Noble as the forest's caretaker, with the understanding that his main job was fire suppression. At first, UK hired local men to fight the fires, but that practice led some locals to set more fires in the hope of landing work (a practice that continues to this day throughout eastern Kentucky, though no longer in Robinson Forest). Only in the late 1930s did the university get the fires under control and begin to actually bring students into the contested watersheds.

I pass through the Mart Bottom clearing and wander farther up Buckhorn Creek. The crooked trunk of an umbrella magnolia seems caught in a decade-old act of indecision, unsure where it should set the single large, white flower that grows at the top of each tree. A large beech tree has fallen onto a gravel bar in the middle of the stream, and the current has slowly sculpted it into a sinuous arch that appears at once very primitive and very modern. Today, however, the stream seems almost indolent as it makes its way down to Troublesome, and it is hard to imagine that this water ever moves with the force that bent the beech. Further on, thirty-foot-tall hop-hornbeam trees line each bank; their crowns touch above the middle of the stream as they lean to catch light coming through the break in the canopy. The creek narrows as I near its confluence with Coles Fork. Jumping from one stone to the next, I cross over the Buckhorn and splash down in the state's cleanest stream.

Thickets of Kentucky's only native cane crowd the banks in places, and hemlocks grow up the sides of the banks. All signs of human trash are gone. The floods have hung matted leaves and sticks in the boughs and branches of trees, but there is no plastic and certainly no Pampers. In fact, there are no signs that humans have been here for some time. The air is cooler and damp. I pass an American hornbeam tree, common to eastern stream banks, and find that a beaver tried to topple it for a dam but apparently abandoned the job halfway through the trunk. The sawyer whose ghost I am tracking today would never even have attempted it. American hornbeam, also called ironwood, is one of the densest trees in this forest, and sawing it is the quickest way to dull a blade. After UK took possession of Robinson Forest, however, there was quite a bit of cutting and clearing here at the mouth of Coles Fork. In 1925 a tent camp was set up along these banks for the young men who would build a camp headquarters back at Mart Bottom and a zoological laboratory on Clemons Fork. Then, in 1933, the Civilian Conservation Corps (CCC), established as part of Franklin Roosevelt's New Deal, built a more permanent camp at Mart Bottom. According to archaeologist Kim A. McBride, on whose extensive research I am leaning, a number of local boys joined the CCC and began cutting trails and constructing bridges throughout Robinson Forest. They also cleared a total of twenty-five acres for picnic grounds, and one of the largest clearings was here at the mouth of Coles Fork. The CCC finally decamped in 1936, leaving behind fifteen buildings that became Robinson Forest's first classrooms. And because the camp served UK's civil engineering department primarily, Mart Bottom became known as the "engineering bottom."

A few years ago, I was walking along the main road into Camp Robinson with some students when a car pulled up beside us. A woman was driving, and a very elderly man sat in the passenger seat. He was reluctant to speak and did not want to get out of the car. But his daughter explained that they had been traveling for several hours because her father had been a CCC camper in the 1930s and wanted to see Robinson Forest one last time.

As I push on along Coles Fork, I become increasingly entangled in the aftermath of the 2009 flood, which pried quite a few sycamores and beeches from the shallow topsoil along these steep banks. I wrestle through the branches of their fallen crowns or under their trunks for about a mile, then decide to redirect my path over higher ground. About six hundred feet above me stands an impressive rock outcrop that looks like it leads all the way over the ridge and then back down to the upper reaches of Coles Fork. Unfortunately, most of the slopes rise up to their outcrops at a fifty-degree angle. The only way up is on all fours, grasping roots and saplings. But I know the view from the top will be impressive, so I heave myself into the climb. Halfway up I notice rosebay rhododendron growing on the colder north sides of the first, lower escarpments of sandstone mixed with iron oxide. As I climb higher, the boulders flatten into sheer, damp walls where ferns and a modest wildflower called stonecrop cling to small crevices. These massive rocks, 280-million-year-old remnants of an ancient stream, have an impressive, if accidental, architecture. Clumsily I pull myself up through their narrow corridors until I am sprawled on top, panting beside a cluster of tripe lichen.

The sky is clear, and I watch a turkey vulture circle overhead. Once, a few years ago, I fell asleep on one of these high rocks and awoke to see a vulture circling only a few feet above me, having decided to his satisfaction that I was a carcass. Ever since then I have dozed at the top of these outcrops with one eye open for buzzards. But as I watch the black bird riding the high thermals, I realize it isn't a vulture at all but a raven—*Corvus corax*, a famously cerebral bird and a trickster in many mythologies. According to one Hebrew folktale, the ravens disgracefully violated Noah's abstinence policy on the Ark. Ever since then, they have had little to do with human culture and instead have developed intricate avian rites of their own. Naturalist Craig Childs once stumbled on a coven of ravens caching owl feathers under desert rocks in a ceremony of ritualistic revenge that certainly sounds very Old Testament. Justice, Childs deduced, was clearly being served—at least according to the corvid morality code. Ravens nest only where humans do not, and today there is no one up here but the raven and me.

I can, however, hear the raspy song of the mountain chorus frogs emanating from the shallow pools down below me. I lie back against the sandstone and my mind wanders to the title of James Still's beautiful

1940 novel *River of Earth*, which is set here on the Cumberland Plateau. I try to convince myself that in fact I am floating on top of a wave. And it's true—in geological time. According to the nearly incomprehensible span that geologists call "deep time," these rocks really are creeping, slowly, through millions of years, down to Coles Fork.

I rise and start walking again along the thin razorback until it descends into a gently sloping saddle. Three impressive shagbark hickories stand like quiet sentries among a few boulders covered by deep green moss. Perhaps eighty years old, the hickories represent the second-growth forest that reemerged after Mowbray-Robinson's logging. These trees don't have the girth of the ones that company hauled away, of course. And there seems to be little agreement on how old an "old-growth forest" has to be. But semantics aside, here is the important fact about Robinson Forest today: *it is one of the last and largest examples of the oldest, most biologically diverse ecosystem in North America—the mixed mesophytic.* That term was coined by an intrepid botanist named Lucy Braun. Born in Cincinnati in 1889, Braun became a pioneer in the emerging study of forest ecology. She bought her first car in 1934, and with her sister Annette traveled sixty-five thousand miles cataloging plants and trees throughout the eastern broadleaf forests. Her favorite region was this one, central Appalachia, where she identified more than eighty species of trees and proposed the term "mixed mesophytic" to describe a forest that is "middling"—not too hot or cold, too wet or dry—and extremely diverse in species. No single species ever dominates the forest canopy. Braun (who pronounced her name "Brown") retired from the University of Cincinnati in 1948, and in 1950 published her seminal work, *Deciduous Forests of Eastern North America.* In it, Braun advanced her theory that when the glaciers moved south during the Pleistocene, central Appalachia became, in her word, a "refuge" of survival for deciduous forest communities. When the glaciers retreated, Braun argued, this part of Appalachia was responsible for repopulating the eastern United States. But no region ever became as biologically diverse as the forest where I am standing.

As I wander down the ridge side, I notice bare spots where wild turkeys have been scratching through the fallen leaves. Farther down I cross a narrow deer path that threads through the beeches and hemlocks. Not far from there I find coyote scat covered by a thin gauze of deer hair. Then, finally back at Coles Fork, I cross over to the wider human route, which the forest looks to be quickly taking over for its own purposes. In some places the former road is already thick with rhododendron. I climb through the dense branches, then cross the creek again, into an embouchure where Panther Branch feeds into Coles Fork. The floods deposited another large sand flat here. This too turns out to be a heavily traveled corridor, and the tracks of turkeys, coyotes, deer, and bobcats are easy to make out in the moist loam.

Up ahead, the stream gurgles around rocks that time has gradually delivered down to this valley floor. Iron-rich rocks on the streambed beneath the gentle current bear a deep crimson hue. Many years ago, Kentucky historian laureate Thomas D. Clark compared a similar body of water to a "frolicksome mountain lass." These days, we hesitate to use such adventurous language, but I think of that phrase as I watch Coles Fork disappear around a bend, and it still seems apt.

Because the Appalachian valleys are so narrow, a stream such as Coles Fork forces both the walker and the logger to follow its own serpentine course—to meander. The word comes from a Greek river known as the Maiandros of Phrygia. With a wandering patience, it flows in wide loops and oxbows down to the Aegean Sea. Here too, Coles Fork takes its time finding its way down to Troublesome Creek. The old logging road keeps crossing back and forth over the stream. Sycamores tilt over the water from the banks. In some places the streambed is sandstone bedrock; in others it is lined with sandstone and cobble. The farther I walk upstream, the more coal I find along the bottom—sleek, almost iridescent blocks worn smooth by the current. Which raises a small question: was this stream originally called Coal Fork, or Coal's Fork? There were, after all, no families named Coles living around here in the 1800s; tax records show them all living twenty miles away in Jackson. And according to a 1990 archaeological report compiled by Tom Sussenbach, some early maps do identify this tributary as Coal's Fork. Whatever the case, the coal in this stream is the reason why Robinson Forest is an embattled wilderness. There are an estimated ninety-seven million tons of the bituminous ore beneath the forest. When E. O. Robinson conveyed the mineral rights of the forest to UK and to then-president Frank L. McVey in 1930, he believed he was eliminating "any possibility that coal mining operations will interfere with the development of the forest"; but he was mistaken.

In the early 1980s, UK considered selling all of the mineral rights to generate revenue. UK forestry major Ann Phillippi was instrumental in forming a group called Students to Save Robinson Forest. The students held rallies, made speeches, and printed up green SAVE ROBINSON FOREST bumper stickers. And in 1983, those students, with the assistance of Sierra Club lawyer Hank Graddy, convinced the UK Board of Trustees that Robinson Forest was too ecologically valuable to mine. Ann Phillippi warned, though, that the specter of mining within the forest would arise again if the land were not legally deemed unsuitable for mining.

She was right. Seven years later, on February 15, 1990, Students to Save Robinson Forest coalesced again in response to Arch Mineral's application to strip-mine 105 acres at the head of Clemons Fork. More bumper stickers were printed up; more rallies were held. This time the Kentucky Resource Council, led by the redoubtable environmental lawyer Tom FitzGerald, petitioned the state's Natural Resources Cabinet to designate the main block of Robinson Forest "land unsuitable for mining." That phrase derives from the 1977 Surface Mining Control and Reclamation Act (SMCRA), which says that strip mining can be legally banned if it can be demonstrated that the mining would destroy competing land interests. The problem was that the Kentucky Natural Resources Cabinet had issued only one such designation since 1982. On March 6, 1990, the UK Board of Trustees signed on to FitzGerald's petition.

Meanwhile, over in Jackson, Arch Mineral organized a counter-rally. Employees and family members carried placards that read: "Research doesn't buy baby food." Arch's chairman, Gene Samples, took the curious but predictable step of blaming 250 recent layoffs at Arch on the Students to Save Robinson Forest. The next month, the Natural Resources Cabinet surprised everyone by ruling that 10,400 acres of the forest's main block was legally unsuitable for mining. As a compromise, UK and the Kentucky Resource Council dropped their efforts to block Arch from mining the 105 acres in question. Not that Arch rehired the 250 laid-off workers. The market was soft, a spokesman explained, and the Tennessee

Valley Authority might buy its coal somewhere else if Arch's price was too high. This would be far from the last time coal operators shifted the blame for lost jobs away from the real cause—their own drive toward increased mechanization and increased profits.

But the victory that preserved the main block of Robinson Forest had an odd effect. It spurred UK to sell the mineral rights to all of the outlying parts of the forest that were not protected. The profits were to be used to support a progressive scholarship program in eastern Kentucky. The Robinson Scholars Program offers full four-year scholarships to one first-generation college student from each of Kentucky's twenty-nine eastern counties. But predictions about coal production in Robinson Forest were over-optimistic, and the $37 million that UK did earn was badly mismanaged. By 2003 the Robinson Scholars endowment was earning less than it cost to sustain the program. The solution, coal operators were quick to point out, was to mine more of Robinson Forest. "What is more important," they argued, "trees or young people?"

Another fight over the fate of Robinson Forest ensued. Another student group was formed; SAVE ROBINSON FOREST bumper stickers once again decorated cars around Lexington. And again the students succeeded. Facing the Robinson Forest controversy for the first time, new UK president Lee Todd said he had no plans to pursue mining there—"at this time." And that caveat underscores an unfortunate reality when it comes to the fight over Robinson Forest: what looks like an environmental victory is too often only the postponement of some final, irrevocable loss.

A hundred years before I was born, on the first day of September 1867, a self-possessed young man named John Muir began his now-famous thousand-mile walk to the Gulf of Mexico in my hometown, Louisville, Kentucky. He recalled that he "steered through the big city by compass without speaking a word to any one." He reached the Cumberland Mountains ten days later. Like a true Scotsman he brought along with him two books, the Bible and Robert Burns' poems; he also carried a plant press for collecting specimens. One night, a blacksmith and his wife took Muir in. When the mountaineer learned that Muir was simply botanizing in his own employ, he remarked, "Picking up blossoms doesn't seem to be a man's work at all." Muir resorted to his Bible, asking the blacksmith, "Now, whose advice am I to take, yours or Christ's. Christ says, 'Consider the lilies.' You say, 'Don't consider them.'" This evidently satisfied the blacksmith, who, Muir reported, "repeated again and again that I must be a very strong-minded man, and admitted that no doubt I was fully justified in picking up blossoms."

We tend to think of John Muir as the celebrator and protector of the American West. But in that first book, *A Thousand-Mile Walk to the Gulf*, he could hardly stop praising the Cumberland Mountains. The Kentucky oaks were the most beautiful he had ever seen, the Clinch River seemed to flow right out of Eden, and the rock shelters were the "most heavenly places" he had ever dropped his pack. "Such an ocean of wooded, waving, swelling mountain beauty and grandeur is not to be described," but he tried. The "sylvan pages" could be read—must be read—as a divine scripture, or what Henry David Thoreau had earlier called the poem of creation.

I find myself wishing, on some level, that Muir had lingered a bit longer in the East and fought to preserve the Appalachian Mountains the way he fought for the western rivers and ranges. I wish he had lavished more of his intoxicating prose on the Cumberlands, awakening more Kentuckians to the *value* of places like Robinson Forest, a value that has nothing to do with the price of timber or a short ton of coal.

But once John Muir saw the sublime glaciers of Yosemite, there was no going back. And perhaps herein lies part of our problem as Easterners. Because the Appalachian Mountains are older than their western counterparts, they are lower, more worn down. They don't possess the vaulting grandeur of the snow-capped Rockies or the plunging cataracts of the Sierra Nevada. They are easier to take for granted; and that, I think, makes them easier to exploit. Ansel Adams calendars and Disney films such as *Earth* and *Oceans* have given us a rather one-dimensional view of the natural world. If it isn't spectacular or dramatic, it isn't interesting. I may never see a coyote ripping apart a deer in Robinson Forest, but neither do I wish to see bulldozers gouging its hillsides for coal. The beauty and value of Robinson Forest are far too subtle for any camera crew to fully document, much less communicate. Instead, the forest is best experienced through what Harvard biologist E. O. Wilson called the "naturalist's trance," in which the experience of a particular place redirects one's attention and curiosity to the natural world. That experience can lead to many things: restoration of psychic equilibrium, a better understanding of native flora and fauna, a sense of reverence for something human beings did not create. All of these experiences are valuable in ways that cannot be quantified with a price. To think of Robinson Forest as only a "natural resource" is to diminish not only it but us—to sacrifice our higher principles.

To walk through Robinson Forest is to experience, or at least to avail oneself to, the only four kinds of knowledge I know: the ethical, scientific, aesthetic, and spiritual. They do not necessarily lead from one to the other. A person, for instance, can gain a greater aesthetic appreciation through knowing the forest's botany, or the aesthetic experience can lead one to pursue a better scientific understanding of these watersheds. I have certainly watched many students experience Robinson Forest aesthetically, scientifically, and spiritually, and I have seen those levels of knowledge lead students to act on an *ethic* to preserve Robinson Forest. "All ethics so far evolved," wrote Aldo Leopold, "rest upon a single premise: that the individual is a member of a community of interdependent parts." The Coles Fork watershed is a perfect example of such a land community; the strip mines to the south are just the opposite—the work of rapacious humans who sacrifice the community's clean air and clean water in the name of profit. That is to say, they have raided the state's common wealth at the expense of their neighbors, and in doing so have radically debased the ethical concept of community. And really, it is a very simple concept. Leopold laid it out for us sixty years ago, and I do not think his formula has been improved: "A thing is right when it tends to preserve the integrity, stability, and beauty of the biotic community. It is wrong when it does otherwise." Any decision to extract natural resources from Robinson Forest should be preceded by this question: Will such extraction harm the beauty, stability, and integrity of these watersheds? If the answer is yes, the decision should be no.

A mile or so farther upstream, beside a copse of American hornbeam trees, I come upon the tallest mountain laurel I have ever seen. These gnarled trees are usually only chest-high, but this one is nearly twenty feet tall and would surely qualify as old growth. I imagine E. O. Robinson finding this spindly mountain laurel in bloom, fluted pink-and-white buds open to the sun, and thinking it too worthless to remove or too beautiful or both. So here it stands still.

A tall beech has fallen across the stream, so I shimmy across and pick up the trail once more under a willowy canopy of hemlocks. The sun is now directly overhead, and the shadows of high branches flicker across the surface of the water. In the quiet, deeper pools, water striders dart like electrons across the surface. In most cases the insects are paired, the male riding on the female's back. Small translucent fish swim in the shadows of their courtship rituals.

I walk on beneath a canopy of beech and hemlock. Soon the road virtually disappears, which I take to be a good sign: I must be getting close to the headwaters. When the road is only a footpath winding through high grass, I see it. Up on a small bluff, about fifteen feet above the river, stands an old stone chimney. I circle around the back side of it and then come into the clearing where the cabin once stood. The keystone still holds the entire hearth intact. Though most of the chinking is gone, not a single stone is missing. The logs of the cabin have disappeared, but the chimney remains, a lonely stalwart at the edge of civilization. Opposite the fireplace itself, a final stream comes trickling into Coles Fork. It falls in gentle gradations down a wide stretch of bedrock and into the larger body of water. The two streams frame this old homestead nicely, and I can understand why the sawyer chose this spot to stake his small claim in the world.

The whole clearing is covered by club moss, a lycopod with waxy green leaves that is one of the last remnant species of the huge *Lepidodendron* trees that flourished in the Pennsylvanian period. When they died, the trees fell into bogs, and over 350 million years were compressed into the black ore that provides more than half of America's electricity. Today's club moss stands about four inches tall and resembles a dense carpet. I lie down to rest and think about the life of the man who once lived here.

He raised a small garden on the land closest to the stream, where the sun peers over the trees. I know this because Andrew Marshall Jr., the son of William Marshall, who married the daughter of one of the first homesteaders in Robinson Forest, told Jim Krupa, who told me. "Junior" also told Jim that the sawyer would walk down to the Mowbray-Robinson mill and pick up blades that needed sharpening. He carried them back here on some beast of burden and went to work. A few days later, he loaded up the sharpened saws and headed back downstream.

I might have learned much more, but Junior died unexpectedly, in a tragic manner, in 2009. He was probably the last living source of information about the sawyer, and about much else concerning Robinson Forest. That local knowledge is now lost. So with nothing else to go on, I try to imagine the life of the man who made his home in this primitive bower. I suspect that after Robinson paid him for his work, the sawyer went on up to Quicksand to buy coffee, salt, flour, and whatever else he couldn't hunt or grow. According to Tom Sussenbach's archaeological report, Robinson's logging roads had made that trip quicker and easier. Perhaps he played a fiddle and knew the old mountain songs like "Bullfrog on a Puncheon Floor." Probably he had planed down split logs to make a puncheon floor for his cabin. He would have bathed in the shallow tributary that ran beside the cabin. And I feel sure that he made a little moonshine. What a pleasure it must have been to sit on his cabin porch at dusk, sip whiskey, and watch a kingfisher patrol Coles Fork from above.

I don't mean to romanticize the sawyer's life. Certainly it was hard. He wouldn't have had much formal education, and he wouldn't have needed it. Still, I like to think that he possessed a rich inner life—that he drew sustenance from this landscape, that he chose this particular place to dwell because it spoke to a deep longing and gave him deep satisfaction. Here, he enacted a kind of wild domesticity that is almost lost to us now.

I stand and gaze upstream to the place where Coles Fork finally buries its head beneath the Cumberland Plateau. According to the Roman poet Virgil, when Aeneas reached the source of the Tiber River, the site of what would become Rome, he found a spectacular forest. Aeneas' host, Evander, explained to him that "a race of men came / From tree trunks, from hard oak." I like that idea—a race of humans born of oaks, descended from a forest not unlike the one where I am standing. The

Romans were not exiles cast out of a garden, but a race that felt John Muir's familial attachment to the flora and fauna of the deep woods.

In the end, of course, the imperial Romans destroyed their forests by turning trees into warships. It could also be argued that they destroyed themselves—that the deforestation represented one more symptom of the unseeing madness of empire. American political scientists and commentators these days ask, "Are we Rome?" Have we, in our rapacious hunger for resources, extended the American empire to the point of economic and ecological collapse? Are we hovering at what many climatologists call a tipping point, beyond which our lives and our planet cannot recover? More than a thousand pages of evidence in the latest report from the United Nations' Intergovernmental Panel on Climate Change suggest we are. June 2012 was the thirty-second consecutive month in which temperatures exceeded the twentieth-century average. In addition, the U.N. Millennium Ecosystem Assessment, carried out between 2001 and 2005, found that human activity has degraded 60 percent of the world's ecosystem services, such as climate regulation, fresh water, air, and water purification, to unsustainable levels. Perhaps the God of the Old Testament should have put the ravens in charge.

I sometimes imagine John Muir taking his thousand-mile walk today. He would begin here among Appalachia's toxic streams and decapitated mountains and end at a Gulf of Mexico that we nearly destroyed with our hubris and spewing oil. And it would not be lost on him that unregulated coal and oil barons are to blame—as are we, the individuals who so conspicuously consume those fossil fuels. For one hundred years we have manufactured and enjoyed an economy based on dishonest accounting and shortsighted borrowing of natural assets from future generations. Cormac McCarthy's postapocalyptic novel *The Road* paints a cold and gray picture of what that future might look like. And it is evident on close reading that the unnamed father and son who encounter hordes of cannibals and sociopaths on their own walk to the Gulf are following the same path Muir took. They find evidence of native Appalachian flora such as ginseng, mayapple, and morel mushrooms; they even pass a SEE ROCK CITY sign painted on a crumbling barn roof. But when they reach the Gulf, they do not find what Muir called "the immortal truth and immortal beauty of Nature." They see instead a lifeless, colorless world that more closely resembles the oil-deadened aftermath of the BP drilling disaster.

UK presidents and UK trustees have many times asked the question they will certainly ask again, "Should we mine Robinson Forest?" Even the asking implies that we have learned very little from the last century of ruinous extraction. It implies that we have much to learn if we are to make it to the end of this century—if we can reclaim some of John Muir's world and stave off the nightmare of Cormac McCarthy's.

CHAPTER 2

Ridgetops and Outcrops

James J. Krupa

Robinson Forest is in a geological region known as the Cumberland Plateau, and in the Eastern Kentucky Coal Field, named for the layers of bituminous coal beneath the surface. The Cumberland Plateau runs along the western edge of the Appalachian Mountains from Kentucky, Virginia, and West Virginia down through Tennessee into Georgia and Alabama. The rock strata exposed in the plateau date back more than 320 million years and are tied to the formation of the Appalachian Mountains.

Although old and weathered now, the Appalachians may once have been as impressive and imposing as the Himalayas are today. They were created in the Paleozoic era over a period of tens of millions of years as the continental plates underlying modern-day Europe, Africa, and South America pushed against the North American plate, causing the eastern edge of the North American plate to buckle and break. Some parts of the colliding plates were thrust up and over others to form a mountain range, an event that geologists call the Appalachian or Alleghanian Orogeny. It is amazing to think that these mountains formed before mammals and dinosaurs evolved. Flowering plants did not exist. Amphibians were the ruling vertebrates, and reptiles were just beginning their rise toward dominance.

The higher and steeper mountains are, the faster they erode. Great volumes of sediment from the erosion of the western Appalachians flowed west in ancient rivers toward a shallow inland sea. As sea levels rose and fell, the inland sea repeatedly advanced toward the Appalachians and then retreated back to the margin of the continent. For millions of years the region of the Cumberland Plateau alternated from shallow sea to coastal deltas and lagoons, to rivers and floodplains, to swamps and forests, and back again. Sediment from these varied environments accumulated in a subsiding basin west of the mountains that is known as the Appalachian Basin. When swamps covered the region, the Cumberland Plateau was hot and humid, lush and green. Ferns and horsetail rushes choked the ground, and scale trees (giant club mosses) and tree ferns filled the canopy above. The swamp water, highly acidic and lacking in oxygen, was hostile to microbial decomposers. When plants and trees died and sank or toppled into the water, they did not decompose as they would today. The dead vegetation slowly transformed into spongy brown peat instead. Sediment left by rivers, coastal deltas and shallow lagoons, and muds of the inland sea eventually covered the peat swamps. With pressure and time the peat transformed into bituminous coal; the coastal and delta sands became sandstone; and the floodplain, lagoon, and shallow sea muds became shale. Layer upon layer was deposited and buried in the subsiding basin as the inland sea advanced and retreated. The fossils from the ancient seas, coastlines, floodplains, and swamps found in the rock layers of the modern forest attest to the repeated advances and retreats.

One can get a feel for what these swamps were like by visiting the Okefenokee Swamp in southern Georgia. Floating mats of peat form islands that cover the swamp and are home to water tupelos, swamp tupelos, and sweet gums. Hundred-foot-tall bald cypress and pond cypress trees tower over the islands. Shrubs such as cyrilia, buttonbush, fetterbush, and dahoon holly fill the understory. Spanish moss hangs from the trees, and water lilies fill the open water. The peat that lies beneath the Okefenokee makes the water acidic and stains it the color of tea. Trees fall and shrubs die, and they do not decay but transform into brown peat, just as the Paleozoic vegetation did in the Appalachian Basin.

I have walked the tree islands of the Okefenokee. Even during the dry season they are a challenge to navigate. The peat is deep, soggy, and soft. Dead logs and tree branches litter the ground and are buried under the brown muck. What looks like firm ground can quickly transform into cold, wet ooze. I sank knee-deep, my legs scraped by buried, broken branches on the way down. One stumbles rather than walks over the floating peat. To explore the Okefenokee is to experience the Paleozoic swamps that once covered Robinson Forest. Of course, the plants were different, the creatures in the swamp were different, the climate was different, and the peat was much thicker than can be found in any peat swamp in the United States today, but it would still have been a mucky mess.

After the continents collided at the end of the Paleozoic, they pulled apart from each other during the Mesozoic. Beginning in the Triassic period of the Mesozoic, the landmass that became Europe, Africa, and South America began to pull away from North America, forming the infant Atlantic Ocean. The Appalachian Mountains stood tall but were no longer being thrust upward. For hundreds of millions of years, rains and winds gradually weathered away their jagged peaks. Sea levels rose and fell. Glaciers advanced and retreated. Rocks that were once buried deep beneath the earth's surface were exposed again.

Today, the Cumberland Plateau resembles a massive layer cake many hundreds of feet deep covering twenty-five thousand square miles. The layers of the plateau in and around Robinson Forest have been given names to aid in regional geologic mapping. Geologists lump beds of rocks into regionally mapable units called groups, formations, and members. Distinctive or economically important beds, such as coals, are also named. For example, the Skyline coal zone occurs in the hills of Robinson Forest at approximately fifteen hundred feet above sea level. Below this zone lies the Tiptop coal zone, then the Hindman coal bed, the Hazard coal zone, the Copland coal bed, layer after layer, ending with the oldest seam exposed at the surface, the Whitesburg coal zone, now eight hundred feet above sea level. The Skyline and Tiptop coals are part of the Princess Formation. The Hindman and Hazard coals are part of the Four Corners Formation. The Copland and Whitesburg coal beds are part of the Hyden Formation. These formations are in turn part of the larger Breathitt Group.

Some of the ridgetops 1,520 feet above sea level are formed of Flint Ridge flint. Flint layers can be formed in many different ways. Some flints are the remains of dead organisms—in this case the remains of silica-rich organisms. The Flint Ridge flint appears to have been deposited in a past shallow sea where sponges once thrived. Sponges are unique among animals for having tiny, rodlike silica structures called spicules, which provide their only defense against predators. When sponges die, their bodies decompose, leaving only the silicon dioxide of the spicules behind to accumulate on the seabed. In time, compression of the seabed layer forms a sedimentary layer of flint. Only a few deposits of flint are known on the Cumberland Plateau; the largest is in Robinson Forest on the ridges above the headwaters of Clemons Fork. These deposits are known as Breathitt chert for the county where they were first found.

For the past 200 million years, seeping water and flowing streams have been cutting through layers of the Cumberland Plateau. Water deposited as rain is pulled by gravity from high ground to lower-lying areas. Trickles of water unite to form rivulets that loosen and carry away soil and sand. Rivulets unite to form streamlets. As ever-larger volumes of water unite, streams form and the erosive force of water intensifies. The streams cut through the soft shale and coal, carrying away the debris they loosen. Buried layers of solid sandstone are resistant to water's erosive powers, but water is not to be deterred. It will continue to flow over the sandstone layer hidden beneath the layers of shale and coal. Eventually it finds and fills cracks. In some cases, water flows through natural fractures in the rocks, always eroding away the least resistant spots.

The Cumberland today is a dissected plateau almost devoid of flat surfaces, a maze of deep, V-shaped hollows; steep slopes; and narrow, twisting ridgetops. It comprises some of the most rugged landscape in eastern North America, and those who live there call it "the mountains." To someone looking out over the landscape from Robinson Forest's fire tower, the Cumberland Plateau looks like wave after wave of small mountains. They once extended to the horizon in all directions—before mining companies started to remove mountaintops. Viewed from a low-flying plane, however, the region is clearly a plateau that has been dissected by water and time. It is a challenging place to live because level ground is so scarce. The ridgetops are dry, with no source of water but rain, and little flat surface to support anything more than a small garden. Farmers once cleared the slopes to grow corn, but the topsoil soon eroded away. Farming now is confined to the hollows along streams where enough flat land can be cleared to grow small quantities of crops. Roads, too, are engineering challenges because they must closely follow streambeds. Hollows are subject to annual flooding, and occasionally flash floods destroy roads and gardens and homes.

Robinson Forest, nestled deep within the Cumberland Plateau, consists of a twelve-thousand-acre main block and scattered smaller parcels totaling another two thousand acres. The main block has been exposed to fire, logging, and some mining, yet it is the most pristine part of the forest. The smaller parcels have been or will be surface-mined and logged. I avoid these damaged tracts of land and concentrate my activities on the main block. On a map, Robinson Forest is shaped like a raindrop resting on its side. The rounder, thicker portion to the west is the Clemons Fork watershed. Both the main entrance to the forest and Camp Robinson are located there, and this is where most human activity occurs. Camp Robinson is a cluster of cabins made from the wood of American chestnuts killed by the blight of the 1920s and 1930s. Students and researchers stay there while working in the forest. Most of the jeep trails that see any use are in this watershed. To the east, the forest is long and narrows almost to a point. This is the Coles Fork watershed, the most pristine portion of the forest where humans rarely go. The road along the stream is no longer drivable, and fallen trees block most of the jeep trails along the ridgetops. The Coles Fork watershed represents the full magnificence and beauty that is Robinson Forest, and it is where I roam alone to escape humanity.

Robinson Forest is hard to get to know. Climbing the steep slopes is exhausting. Hiking up hollows and along streambeds is slow and difficult work. Fallen trees litter the hollow bottoms, crisscross streambeds, and block the seldom-used jeep trails. Climbing over the tree trunks or crawling under them is a bruising business. This forbidding toughness is what makes Robinson Forest a unique place to work. Nowhere else in

Kentucky do I find the serenity and solitude I experience when I am deep in the Coles Fork watershed.

Scattered along the ridgetops of Robinson Forest are isolated sandstone outcrops that were deposited in the Paleozoic and withstood the weathering force of later streams. They contain naturally cemented quartz grains and iron oxides, which are more resistant to erosion than some of the underlying and overlaying rock layers. As the shale and topsoil along the ridgetops weather away, the sandstone formations become more exposed and pronounced. Each of these formations is a unique, naturally sculptured piece of art, a monument to some ancient event, shaped by wind and rain, freezing and thawing, expansion and contraction. Some are massive piles of boulders and blocks stacked precariously one atop the other with large gaps and arches in between. Some are solid formations more than fifty feet tall and extending three hundred feet along the ridge. Others are filled with fractures and crevices that are vertical, horizontal, or diagonal.

Crevices can be wide or narrow, deep or shallow, and their size, number, and angles differ from one outcrop to the next. Some crevices extend all the way through an outcrop; others lead to a dead end. A few outcrops have shallow caves and deep rock shelters that are cool, dark, and dry. I have taken refuge in these on many occasions, remaining dry and comfortable while waiting for thunderstorms to pass. They provide refuge for other creatures as well. In the summer, single male Rafinesque's big-eared bats roost in them. Bobcats, gray foxes, and coyotes take refuge during the day, leaving behind footprints as proof of their recent visits. Some of the rock shelters are substantial, with ceilings formed from sandstone overhangs several feet above the shelter floor. Humans have taken refuge in these shelters for eight thousand years.

The prehistoric inhabitants cared nothing for the seams of coal beneath the outcrops that modern humans covet. They valued the sandstone and flint they found there. Sandstone provided rock shelters; flint provided the raw materials for making projectile points. Without them, survival and hunting would have been very difficult. More than fifty of the rock shelters in the forest contain evidence that prehistoric hunter-gatherers spent time in them. Some have campfire rings made of sandstone in which pieces of charcoal still remain; others have large, flat rocks with smooth, circular depressions that prehistoric visitors used as grinding platforms. Flint chips scattered about the floor beneath a layer of dust provide evidence that projectile points were once produced there. Although it is clear that ancient humans spent extended periods in these shelters, the lack of clay pottery suggests that they did not take up permanent residence in Robinson Forest. Yet they spent enough time and had enough free time to etch symbols into the sandstone, and some of these petroglyphs still exist.

As a naturalist, I am intrigued by the individuality of Robinson's outcrops. As a biologist, I am fascinated by the biodiversity each supports. As an ecologist, I am amazed that each is a separate ecosystem, an isolated habitat island different from all the others. Each outcrop has a unique microclimate and supports an assemblage of species found nowhere else in the forest. Assemblages that thrive on outcrops could not exist on forest floors or on the trunks of giant oaks. Cool, wet, shady north-facing sandstone is where rock-loving ferns grow. Rosebay rhododendrons typically thrive along cool, shaded stream banks. They rarely occur on the dry, hot ridgetops—except where there are large outcrops with expansive north-facing sides and water seeps. Here the microclimate is wetter and cooler than anywhere else on the ridgetops, and moisture-loving plants typically found deep in the hollows can survive. Dense stands of rosebay rhododendrons hug some outcrops; dense tangles of branches sprout from the sandstone's base. Maidenhair spleenwort, mountain spleenwort, walking ferns, rock cap ferns, and common polypody grow out from soil-filled cracks in vertical surfaces. The warmer, drier sides of outcrops are more challenging for plants. After the leaves have fallen to the forest floor and the canopy is bare, sunlight dries the outcrops; these intermittent dry periods challenge the survival of photosynthetic organisms. Lichens and mosses have evolved adaptations to deal with the periods of desiccation: they become dormant. Reproduction stops and growth ceases. It might seem that these photosynthetic organisms would prefer less hostile conditions, but lichens and mosses growing on the forest floor would be buried by leaf litter and die without access to the sun's rays. Those trying to grow on wet, cool rocks down in the hollows would be outcompeted by larger, faster-growing plants. Growing on hot, dry rocks is thus a successful evolutionary strategy as long as the organism can withstand weeks, months, and even years of dormancy and desiccation. Dozens of species of lichens and mosses can do just that, and consequently the vertical surfaces of Robinson Forest's outcrops are covered with many colonies of the drought-tolerant rock dwellers.

Lichens and mosses are also creative in the ways they avoid competition with other lichens and mosses. Many species grow only on the bark of specific species of trees. Some grow only on oaks, others on ash or maples. Some species grow on a specific type of rock—sandstone, shale, limestone, or flint—while others grow on rock of any type. The more specific their ecological niche, the less they have to compete with other lichens and mosses. Each outcrop in Robinson Forest is a unique microcosm of communities of sandstone-loving lichens and mosses, and each is splashed with colors in a unique combination depending on the species that make up that particular community: mosses of every conceivable shade of green; lichens that are many shades of green as well, but also black, brown, gray, yellow, orange, blue-green, and red. Many species form a thin crust tightly fused to the stone; others are large, brittle flakes barely attached. The names of the lichens growing on the outcrops are as diverse as their colors and tell much about their appearance: cowpie lichen, crater lichen, rock greenshield, rock shingle, common toadskin, blackened toadskin, fluffy dust lichen, rock axil-bristle, crottle, salted shield lichen, spotted wart, rock wart, stipplescale, Cumberland rockshield, Plitt's rock-shield, green reindeer lichen, and gray reindeer lichen.

Lichens are biological oddities. Each has a unique scientific name as though it were a single organism, yet each lichen is actually two species living in a symbiotic relationship so dependent on each other that they cannot survive on their own. One symbiont is always a fungus that provides the architectural structure and support; the other species is either a photosynthetic bacterium or an alga that makes food for both. This type of symbiotic relationship has existed for hundreds of millions of years. Lichens grow slowly and are capable of living more than a hundred years. They are desiccated and dormant for a significant portion of that time, but alive nonetheless. Lichens are the champions of resiliency. Some that were plucked from rock, glued to a piece of cardboard, and shoved into a herbarium case where they sat in total darkness free of moisture for more than twenty years sprang back to life when misted and exposed to sunlight.

The oddest of Robinson Forest's lichens are the two rock tripes (plated and smooth). They grow only on vertical faces of outcrops, but there they dominate. During most of the year, rock tripe does not resemble the pig's rubbery stomach lining for which it is named. Rather, each "individual" looks like a dried, shriveled leaf glued to the stone. The underside is black, and the light brown surface crumbles away when touched. Gaps of exposed sandstone occur between each individual. When it rains, rock tripe undergoes a rapid and drastic transformation. Each "shriveled leaf" quickly absorbs water and expands to many times its dormant size. It becomes thin and rubbery, and really does look like a piece of tripe sagging from the outcrop at its point of attachment. The surface turns rich olive green as the chloroplasts are activated and photosynthesis resumes. A photosynthesizing colony of rock tripe can cover an outcrop, making it look green and alive. The lichen consumes rainwater and carbon dioxide, releases oxygen, and produces sugar. With photosynthesis comes growth, and the chemical processes involved release acids that bit by bit dissolve the sandstone beneath the lichen. Slowly, over millennia, lichens gnaw away at their substrate, turning sandstone into mineral soil. The sides of some outcrops have concavities the size of dinner plates where lichens have been wearing down the rock. After the rain and clouds depart, the outcrop slowly dries, photosynthesis grinds to a halt, and the rock tripe withers back to its crusty dormant state. It will remain dormant until the next rain.

Mosses can successfully compete with lichens for space on the vertical faces of outcrops, but they dominate the horizontal surfaces atop rock formations. Here they hold moisture, minerals, and organic nutrients in place beneath their dense green carpets. Like lichens, mosses can handle desiccation. They can cope with conditions fluctuating from hot to cold, and from wet to dry. They also release acids as they grow, slowly dissolving the top of the outcrop to form a mineral-rich soil on which they thrive. All the while, the moisture they hold beneath the green carpet freezes and thaws, chipping away at the sandstone and forming tiny crevices. These fill with water, and when the temperature drops below freezing, the water forms ice crystals that act as wedges, splitting the crevice wider and deeper. Soil fills the widening cracks, and soon tender young serviceberry roots grow into the crevices in search of precious nutrients. The roots grow, also releasing acids, and press against the walls of the crevice, leading to a phenomenon called "root pry," which accelerates the widening of crevices into cracks and then into fractures. Lichens and mosses continue their slow, relentless assault on the outcrop. Eventually, after tens of thousands or hundreds of thousands of years, the outcrop will succumb and crumble away. With this demolition, the lichens and mosses will have destroyed the structure on which they exist and will die. Survival of the species depends on their spores colonizing younger outcrops and boulders elsewhere in Robinson Forest.

I have spent years exploring Robinson Forest with the goal of finding every outcrop in the forest, in particular the ones that provide a suitable dwelling place for mammals. I have hiked up every hollow and along every stream. I have walked all the ridgetops and scrambled up all of the slopes. It took me years to accomplish this. I am one of the very few people alive today who has walked all of Robinson Forest. Some of the outcrops had already been identified and named during the 1981 survey to prepare the forest's most recent topographic map, but most of them I had to find by myself. The dense green leaves and deep shade of summer hide the rock formations, and you can pass within a few feet of one and never see it. The best time to find outcrops is from late November to mid-March, when the leaves have fallen and the forest becomes three-dimensional. I have spent hours in the fire tower in the dead of winter scanning the forest with binoculars and looking for anything resembling a big rock. Sunny winter days following fresh snowfall are best for hunting outcrops. I have walked the ridges scanning adjacent ridges and slopes. Even in winter, though, an outcrop can be missed. Overcast days reduce everything in the forest to varying shades of brown and gray. The colorful lichens seem faded when viewed from a distance. The vertical profiles of trees obliterate the outlines of outcrops. Most of the outcrops required sweat, persistence, determination, and occasionally blood to find.

After eighteen months hiking the forest, I took to the air to look for outcrops. Kentucky Fish and Wildlife and the Rocky Mountain Elk Foundation reintroduced elk onto the reclaimed surface mines of the Cumberland Plateau in 1997, and this generated research funding for wildlife biologists studying elk population dynamics and reproduction. David Maehr, a wildlife biologist at the University of Kentucky, had a cadre of graduate students studying large mammals. Jeff Larkin was one of them. Jeff was studying elk on the reclaimed mines surrounding Robinson Forest, and he spent a lot of time in Cessnas tracking radio-collared animals. He agreed to let me tag along to help spot elk from the plane; in return, we would fly over Robinson to locate outcrops. My first such outing is not a pleasant memory.

On a clear, calm April morning in 1999, I waited at the Bluegrass Airport in Lexington, Kentucky, for my ride. Soon a single-engine Cessna 172 dropped out of the bright blue sky to collect me. Mark Clemons, the pilot, had flown in from Frankfort. Mark was a seasoned pilot and Vietnam War veteran under contract to the state to fly wildlife biologists over their study sites. I climbed aboard eagerly, and we took off toward Stanton, Kentucky, to pick up Jeff. I love being in small planes. They fly slower and closer to the ground than commercial airliners, giving the opportunity to study the landscape below in detail.

On the way to Stanton I kept my face plastered to the window studying every tree, river, and stream below. Mark noticed and asked me if I was feeling okay. I told him I was having a great time and loving the view. Mark decided it was time to prepare me for the day and told me he got hazard pay for flying wildlife biologists to radio track elk and bears. He watched my reaction. I nodded; that's interesting. Mark then asked me if I knew that small plane crashes were the leading cause of death for wildlife biologists. I nodded again; yes, I had heard that. Finally, Mark said, "You know this is going to be a wild ride?" In response, I uttered three words spoken only by fools: "Bring it on!" Mark merely smiled. He turned his attention back to flying, and I went back to studying the landscape below.

As we neared Jeff's study site, Robinson Forest came into view. It's hard to miss from the air. Robinson is a rugged green island surrounded by a gray sea of active and reclaimed surface mines. Sunlight passing through the translucent new leaves gave the forest a bright green glow that day. Robinson has more relief than the surrounding landscape as well. Mountaintop removal involves cutting off ridgetops and dumping the "overburden" into the hollows below, so reclaimed mines look flat, much like the Cumberland Plateau did 200 million years ago before the hollows began to form. In every way, Robinson stood in stark contrast to the land around it. I had little time to muse on the subject. Jeff was getting his first signal from a collared elk, and it was time to get to work. Mark slowed the engine, and the Cessna began to drop. Not far above the tree line, Mark tilted the right wing toward the ground and sent the Cessna into a tight spiral. Jeff told me to look for the collared elk. After the plane made several circles, I spotted the elk and Jeff was able to identify it based on the frequency of the signal. I was exhilarated. This was fun.

As we began circling over the third elk, Mark went into a new figure-eight maneuver. One moment I was looking down at the ground as the right wing was tilted toward the ground. The next moment I was looking at nothing but blue sky. I quickly shifted from the right-side window to the left to regain my view of the ground. The maneuver made me feel a bit dizzy, but I thought nothing of it. Suddenly the cabin felt very warm. I started to sweat—a cold, clammy sweat. The base of my skull started throbbing, and I felt uneasiness deep in my bowels. It spread to my stomach. I was getting motion sickness. I tried to fight it. I kept saying to myself, "Mind over matter. Mind over matter." The words did not help.

As the plane spiraled over one elk and then another, with an occasional figure-eight thrown in, I felt worse and worse. I lost my enthusiasm for elk, outcrops, and Robinson Forest, and also the will to live. I was dizzy, hot, soaked in cold sweat, and trying to hold onto my breakfast. Finally I lost the battle I had no chance of winning. I fumbled for one of the little brown paper bags saturated with wax and lost my morning meal. That didn't make me feel any better. I felt worse. Dry heaves followed, and I quickly depleted the supply of barf bags. I wanted to be put out of my misery. Mark, fully aware of my battle in the backseat, said, "Man, you couldn't get me in a plane if it made me this sick!" He looked cool and calm, like someone taking a leisurely Sunday drive through scenic countryside in a Buick.

Eventually we needed to land at the tiny Hazard, Kentucky, airport to refuel and restock the barf bag supply. I bent over the restroom sink, splashing cold water on my face. It did not help to look in the mirror. My normally tan face was sickly white. When I staggered out of the restroom, Mark and Jeff offered to locate and mark my outcrops so I could stay in the airport lounge. I refused. It was my project, my responsibility. I crawled back into the Cessna and we flew over Robinson in search of outcrops. Unfortunately, this involved one figure-eight after another. Jeff would get GPS readings for each outcrop, then Mark would veer off to find the next rock. I just lay in the backseat, getting sicker and sicker and unable even to look out the window. I wanted my misery to end—and at that point I didn't care how. Eventually, after another eternity, we landed at the Hazard airport to refuel again. I dragged myself to the restroom and tried splashing cold water on my face again. Fortunately for me, the wind began to pick up and it was no longer safe to spiral over the treetops. It was time to head home. The closer we got to Lexington, the better I felt. I was fine by the time we landed. Mark asked if I would be going up again. I hesitated before saying, "Certainly!" Mark just shook his head and smiled, no doubt remembering my earlier encouragement to "Bring it on!"

Most people who have such an experience never volunteer to do it again, but I have a nasty competitive streak. I had to beat the motion sickness and show Mark I could go up again without getting sick. Fortunately, I discovered Dramamine before I got back in the plane two weeks later. This time I did not get sick. And once I started paying attention, I realized how little a margin of error Mark had as he maneuvered the Cessna over the treetops. I appreciated Mark's flying skill and understood why he got hazard pay for flying biologists over the Cumberland Plateau. We spotted many elk and located several new outcrops in Robinson Forest on that second flight. In all, after two years and many days and nights of searching, I have located and examined 153 outcrops, although I am sure others have escaped me.

For the first fifteen years that I worked in Robinson Forest, I carried an old topographic map folded and stuffed in my backpack. It was my travel guide and constant companion. I spent hours studying the purple contour lines, locations of streams, and positions of hollows. All my research sites were marked on the map: fish collection sites were assigned letters with purple ink, wildlife clearings were numbered and marked with green circles, and sites where I trapped small mammals were labeled with brown letters. As I located outcrops, I entered a red identification code precisely on the appropriate contour line: R1, R36, R52C—one for each of the 153 outcrops I found. The map is old and tattered now, and quite colorful from all my pen and pencil marks and notes. The purple contour lines are badly faded, in some cases smeared by drops of my sweat. The folds are so worn that the map is on the verge of falling apart. It no longer travels with me to the forest and is no longer folded. Now it is properly rolled and kept in a purple cardboard tube, safe and dry on a shelf in my office.

Although all the outcrops are assigned one of my "R" codes, some also have official names assigned by the surveyors in 1981: Johnson Rock, Table Rock, Tip Rock, Shelly Rock, Mart Rock, and Robinson Rock. I have given my favorite outcrops names as well: Bee Rock, Bobcat Rock, Chalet Rock, Ridge Rock, Little Johnson Rock, Big Ass Rock, Little Big Ass Rock, Townhouse Rock, Barf Rock, and Vulture Rock. Each name has significance, although often only I know what it is. Each has a unique shape and a unique ecology. Some have vultures' nests every year. Some are observation posts for gray foxes and barred owls. Some shelter bats or bobcats. Several have soft, moss-covered ledges on which I have observed wildlife and caught the occasional nap. Several with rock shelters have protected me from passing thunderstorms and provided cool shade on hot summer days.

It is exciting to discover a new outcrop and see the particular combination of plants and lichens that grow on it and to determine which animals live in it. I never know what I will find. I hiked by outcrop R31 at least four times without noticing it because it was hidden by a dense stand of rhododendrons. The fifth time, I caught a glimpse of a vertical sandstone face and waded in to investigate. Behind the rhododendrons was a long outcrop that only stood ten feet tall but had a rock shelter deep enough and spacious enough for several people to sit comfortably safe from wind and rain. The ceiling was blackened at one end, and beneath it I saw a circle of stones with pieces of charred wood scattered about. I was ecstatic—convinced I had found an undiscovered prehistoric fire ring. The presence of rusted cans put that hope to rest. Each can still had a jagged-edged lid bent back just enough to let a spoon inside. Disappointed at not finding a prehistoric site, I was nevertheless excited to think this might be a historic site—that ninety years ago some of Mowbray-Robinson's loggers sat around the fire, out of the rain, having a meal of pork and beans. Then I noticed scratches on the shelter wall that told the less enchanting reality: "M., Bob Estep, 51," "U.K., D. K. Arbright, 1951, C.E.," and "Mining, Eugene Brashear, Hazard, '51."

I kept looking, though, and behind the fire ring I found a midden pile—a stack of sticks and twigs mounded up against a crevice—evidence that generations of Allegheny woodrats had occupied the shelter. Fragments of acorns and hickory shells, the remains of past woodrat meals, littered the floor. Fresh green leaves and moist mushrooms indicated a current resident. The woodrat had stacked a nice collection of box turtle shells and rusted cans on top of the midden pile.

The Robinson Forest outcrops are isolated habitat islands, each separated from the next by hundreds of feet, if not by miles. Many other animals in addition to woodrats depend on the outcrops for their survival. Crevices provide shelter—a place to raise young, escape predators, and store food. Male Rafinesque's big-eared bats roost in rock shelters and in deep, wide crevices in the summer, and various bats of the genus *Myotis* wedge into the smallest cracks to hibernate during the winter. I have placed motion-sensitive wildlife cameras in some of the deeper crevices. The camera emits an infrared beam and takes a picture each time a passing creature interrupts the beam. The cameras have revealed a diverse procession of creatures that frequently visit outcrops. One photograph captured a turkey vulture apparently assessing a crevice as a possible nest site. Gray foxes, raccoons, woodchucks, white-footed mice, eastern chipmunks, gray squirrels, woodrats, flying squirrels, and striped skunks all frequently investigate crevices. I have one photo of a curious young bobcat with its nose inches from the lens. It must have been quite shocked by the blinding camera flash. In any event, it did not stay long enough to be photographed a second time. Some of Robinson Forest's rarest mammals have eluded my cameras so far, but I have evidence that they too take refuge in outcrops. I suspect that two of these species, the eastern spotted skunk and the Appalachian cottontail, absolutely depend on them. In time, my wildlife cameras will help me determine if this is so.

No mammal is as dependent on outcrops in Robinson Forest as the Allegheny woodrat, which cannot survive without the complex systems of deep, dry crevices and fractures the outcrops contain. When I tell people I study Allegheny woodrats in Robinson Forest, the response is usually a look of disgust. "Rat" conjures up the image of the Norway rat (*Rattus norvegicus*)—the infamous sewer rat with the long, scaly tail, pointed nose, beady eyes, and coarse dark fur; the creature symbolic of urban filth. That is not my woodrat. The Allegheny woodrat (*Neotoma magister*) has long, soft fur. Its belly is white, most of the body is buffy brown, and the arms have yellowish patches. The tail is furry and two-toned: black above, white below. My woodrat has big black eyes and huge, soft ears. Its nose is not pointed; it ends with a rather bulbous snout that gives the woodrat a comical look. The feet are white with thickly furred toes. Allegheny woodrats are gorgeous creatures!

Woodrats face constant pressure from nature. Consequently, I am very careful not to stress or harm them when live-trapping. I try to make everything for the trapped animal safe and comfortable during the night it spends in the trap. I minimize stress by placing ample cotton in the trap for a soft nest and including apple slices for a fine meal. I wedge the trap into a crevice and hold it in place with rocks so a predator cannot dislodge it, then pack leaves in the crevice around the trap for protection from wind. Flat rocks keep the leaves in place.

When an outcrop provides suitable conditions for woodrats, the evidence is unmistakable, even though the woodrat's nest is never visible. Nests, which are the size and shape of a bowling ball, are where the woodrats sleep and where females raise their young. They are made of soft leaves and built in the deepest, driest, safest crevices. The most preferred outcrops have many horizontal and vertical crevices and fractures, many of them opening onto ledges several feet above the ground. The crevice that holds the nest will have a midden pile positioned where the crevice opens onto the ledge. The woodrat stacks twigs, bark, pinecones, bones, and other collectables—many with no discernible use—onto the midden. The chewed remains of hickory nuts and acorns, piled high on the midden, spill over the ledge and down onto the ground. Other crevices and small ledges are latrines, their function clear from the piles of black droppings, tiny footballs half the size of raisins.

The best outcrops are passed down from one woodrat generation to the next. Each generation adds more debris to the midden pile. In the dry rock shelters, the debris continues to accumulate over decades with little decay. Chalet Rock, high above Ridge Hollow, has a rock shelter with a three-foot ceiling and is nearly filled by a midden twelve feet wide and nearly ceiling height. It is the largest woodrat midden in Robinson Forest. Hundreds of generations of woodrats have probably contributed bark, branches, pinecones, bones, and feathers to it. Middens can be hundreds, even thousands of years old. Woodrats collect objects that they find unusual, especially human trash, the body parts of other creatures, bones, and shiny pieces of metal. Old shotgun shells are a favorite. I dropped a loaded .410 shotgun shell near an outcrop in 1996 and found it on a midden pile in the outcrop seven years later. The shell looked as good as new, suggesting the woodrat collected it soon after I dropped it. I have found American chestnut hulls in middens. The last of Robinson Forest's chestnuts were killed by the blight in 1939, so the hulls had been on the midden for at least seventy years.

Woodrats are curious about their surroundings. I have crawled over outcrops, peering into crevices looking for middens and fresh evidence indicating a current resident, only to be startled to find the woodrat calmly watching me. Walking past outcrops at dusk, I have looked up to see woodrats on ledges above staring down at me. More than once, a woodrat has followed me the length of an outcrop, hopping from ledge to ledge above me. Once I found a rock shelter with a wide fracture extending vertically up through the ceiling. Ten feet up, it was transected by a horizontal crevice that created two ledges facing each other. I was lying on my back, shining a light up through the crevice looking for roosting bats, when I saw the flash of a white belly as a woodrat jumped across from one ledge to the other. Quickly it jumped again. Soon a face and two white feet appeared over the ledge; then two big ears. The woodrat was on her belly, her head over the edge, watching me. We studied each other for five minutes or so until she had seen enough and disappeared. A few weeks later I set traps and caught a large, mature female with a striking amount of yellow fur—one of the largest and most beautiful woodrats I have ever seen in Robinson Forest. I trapped her several times over a two-year period. She seemed to enjoy the apple slices I used for bait. Then she disappeared. Most likely a predator killed her while she was foraging on the forest floor.

Woodrats are fairly safe when they are in their nests deep within crevices. Rat snakes and rattlesnakes are the only predators that can reach them there, although the rustle of leaves and bark that signals a snake's approach through the midden may provide enough warning for the woodrat to escape. But woodrats cannot hide in their nests indefinitely. They all have to venture out to search for food, and males to search for mates. Predators prowl the outcrops, waiting for woodrats to emerge. Adult woodrats are thoroughly familiar with their outcrop and the surrounding forest. They know where the hiding places are beyond the outcrop: hollow logs, holes at the base of living trees, rotted tree trunks with tunnel systems that were once roots. They have multiple escape routes back to their outcrop, and once there, navigate through the outcrop's crevices back to the safety of their nest.

Despite their familiarity with the surrounding forest and the abundance of escape routes, woodrats are in mortal peril when they leave the safety of their home to forage, and every hickory nut or acorn they find requires a separate trip back to the outcrop. Raccoon droppings are common on and around outcrops, and wildlife cameras show that raccoons prowl there nightly. Barred owls strike from above like stealth fighters, without warning. These nocturnal hunters are evolutionary marvels. Their soft feathers absorb sound, and the fringes on the leading and trailing edges of their wings eliminate noise as air streams over and under. Owls have hearing far superior to that of other birds, and keen eyesight as well. Their eyes are directed forward for stereoscopic vision, giving them depth-of-field perception that rivals any primate's. Strong, calcified tendons attach their powerful leg muscles to long, sharp talons that deeply penetrate the prey's body, puncturing vital organs and causing swift death. A woodrat being hunted by a barred owl rarely knows until it is too late.

Aerial threats are not the only problem. Timber rattlesnakes are ambush predators that will sit motionless along a woodrat's escape route for days. An unsuspecting woodrat that happens by had better be moving fast; otherwise, a quick strike will result in venom injected deep into the body followed by quick death. The woodrat had best not follow the same route too often. Rattlesnakes will know. Coyotes, bobcats, and gray foxes are constantly on the prowl for woodrats. They leave their footprints in the dry, powdery soil on the floors of rock shelters. They occasionally pull midden piles apart to expose the crevice that contains the nest. Each night, a woodrat has to weigh its options: stay safe in the outcrop and risk running out of food, or forage on the forest floor and risk being killed? This is the Darwinian struggle for existence faced by every woodrat every night of its life. Eventually, every woodrat loses the struggle.

Further complicating the woodrat's life is the fact that adults simply do not like one another. Each outcrop, no matter its size, has only one adult woodrat. A mother wood rat permits her two to four pups to live with her until they become young adults, but one day she will force them out into the forest. Predators take most of the dispersing youngsters before they discover an outcrop. If the outcrop is already occupied, the youngster will be driven away. Mortality is high for Robinson's young woodrats. This is why there are so few of them in such a large forest, and why so many outcrops that are perfect homes for woodrats remain unoccupied for years.

If a young female successfully finds a suitable outcrop, her days of extended travel have ended—unless a younger, stronger, more aggressive woodrat displaces her. She will stay put and wait for her future mate to find her. Long trips to other outcrops in search of mates are thus a part of life for males. Periodically a male woodrat must leave the safety of his outcrop to travel along the ridgetops of Robinson Forest in search of an outcrop with a female receptive to mating. A male may travel miles, possibly for several days, to arrive at an outcrop, only to find another male living there and ready to defend his rock, or a female that is nonreceptive, or perhaps no woodrat at all. There is much I still do not know about the lives of woodrats in the forest. I really have no idea how far or for how long a male woodrat has to travel to find a receptive female. I have no idea how familiar he is with the forest. The risk of predation must be huge, but I do not know how huge. That most of the outcrops in Robinson Forest have middens with no occupants is indication of how difficult life is for woodrats. When a male does find a receptive female, his visit is short. The two mate, and then the female chases him away. The male has to decide whether to look for more mates or return home. The journey home is just as dangerous as the outward journey, and it may end with the discovery that another woodrat has taken over in his absence. Then even more decisions: fight for the outcrop or search for another?

The female woodrat deals with her pregnancy on her own. Her need for food increases as the embryos grow; she has to venture out more often to forage. After her pups are born, she must produce enough milk to feed them, which requires even more foraging. With luck, her pups will grow and thrive and begin to feed themselves. They will learn how to forage for acorns and hickory nuts, and how to avoid predators. They will stay with the mother until that inevitable day arrives when she forces them out of the outcrop to fend for themselves. Occasionally, adult daughters will remain in some of the largest formations if the crevice system is complex enough. Sons never have this option. For a mother to allow her son to stay means risking inbreeding and the spread of lethal recessive genes. For males and females alike, it is in everyone's best interests for the sons to leave. Some will survive and succeed in finding a new home. Either by luck or by having more acute senses, some in each generation will survive.

Robinson Forest's small population of Allegheny woodrats is holding on by the thinnest of threads. As the forest becomes more of an isolated island in a growing sea of barren "reclaimed" surface mines, the Allegheny woodrat's chances of survival diminish. Forest fragmentation and isolation lead to loss of genetic diversity because woodrats carrying new genes are unable to reach the forest. As the numbers decline, the woodrat population begins to spiral down what ecologists call the "extinction vortex," a chain reaction of events that ends when all the woodrats are gone.

I do not know if the woodrat population in Robinson Forest is stable and healthy, albeit small, or in the extinction vortex. Over a period of two years I trapped all 153 outcrops, some repeatedly, and managed to catch only eighteen woodrats. My gut feeling is that they are in the vortex. I hope I am wrong, but only time will tell. The surrounding destruction of habitat and Robinson's increasing isolation on the Cumberland Plateau does not bode well for the beautiful Allegheny woodrats.

Outcrops, like woodrats, are born, age, and eventually die. Young outcrops exposed by erosion are relatively solid, layered structures with natural cracks and fractures. Freezing and thawing, expansion and contraction, wind and rain lay siege to the rock formation along the natural fractures and cracks. Lichens and mosses slowly gnaw away at the sandstone. More cracks form, and some develop into crevices. Fractures widen. Sand and gravel perpetually crumble free and become part of the soil below. The outcrop develops more and more character as it continues to erode. Oaks, maples, and serviceberries gain a foothold on the great sandstone formations and wedge their small roots into every crack and crevice. Root pry ensues. Acids from the roots help to dissolve the sandstone, and as the roots continue to grow and thicken, they exert more pressure on the widening crevice. The siege may be slow, but it is unrelenting. Over countless thousands of years, the once-solid outcrop will come to resemble a three-dimensional jigsaw puzzle with all the pieces still in place. As time goes by, pieces begin to fall from the puzzle; quartz sand and gravel are pried loose from the rock formation and accumulate at the outcrop's base. Rubble fields comprised of rocks ranging in size from a fist to an office desk grow as pieces of rock fall from between cracks and fractures. Eventually, blocks the size of cars and garages become so fractured from the outcrop that they break free and crash to the forest floor. It is easy to find the spot in the outcrop where the blocks were once inserted. These freed blocks have only begun their next journey, which involves geological creep and slow disintegration as they travel down the slopes toward the streams below. This journey may last tens of thousands, hundreds of thousands, possibly millions of years. Meanwhile, the outcrop left behind will eventually dissolve away into the forest floor. The lichens and mosses will be long gone. The woodrats will have left long ago in search of other outcrops. This is all part of the great geological rock cycle. Sand becomes stone eventually to become sand once again.

CHAPTER 3

A Timbered Classroom

Erik Reece

To be a naturalist is not just an activity but an honorable state of mind.
—E. O. WILSON

One Sunday morning in March, I was driving a truck full of college students up a narrow logging road that runs along the western boundary of Robinson Forest. It was the middle of the spring semester. Back in January, on the first day of "ENG 401: Nature Writing," I had informed the class that there would be a mandatory weekend field trip to Robinson Forest. I wanted this small group of students to experience the forest firsthand, and I was hoping that by writing in an untrammeled natural setting, some of them might experience the minor epiphanies that define Thoreau's writing and that have in many ways come to define this rich American genre of writing.

Before we left campus early that Saturday morning, I told the class there would be a two-day moratorium on complaining. This was a wilderness adventure, of sorts, and they were to embark in an intrepid state of mind. But even so, things didn't start well. I learned when we reached the forest that several of my urban students had serious anxieties about being "stuck" for two days in the wild without TV or cell phone reception. I learned later that one young woman had even tried to convince the friend she was riding with to have a minor accident so they could turn back. No one seemed prepared for the steep slopes that characterize the terrain of central Appalachia. On the first morning, the group had gone only fifty feet up one slope when I heard a voice below say, "Can you get mud off cashmere gloves?"

But by the second day the students were starting to notice things—the different lichens and mosses, the call of a barred owl, the gelatinous eggs of the salamanders that were breeding in small puddles. At night they built a raging fire in the large fire ring at the center of Camp Robinson. Huddled around the flames and with no electronic media to entertain them, they quickly reverted to the ancient tradition of oral storytelling.

On the last morning of our trip, I had all but one of my students squeeze into the back of my pickup. I was driving a badly rutted dirt road shaded by hemlocks, oaks, and hickories. The day was sunny, and the students jammed into the truck bed were laughing and howling in exaggerated pain as the tires hit mud puddles. Riding in the cab with me was an older student named Ben, who always wore a black wool cap and a slightly menacing look in class. He had been in the Marines; after that, he spent eight years repairing d-11 dozers and other large mining equipment in eastern and western Kentucky. He was taking the course only because he needed it to fill a requirement for his degree. He was, in his own words, "a right-wing nut job," and he disagreed with virtually everything I said. But he was also funny and respectful, and I liked having him in the class. And I had the feeling that, despite his better judgment, he was beginning to like me as well.

When I reached the highest-elevation tree community, the oak-pine forest, I turned not into the forest but instead onto the vast plateau of the strip mine that covers hundreds of acres along the northern edge of Robinson Forest. A wide, dusty road led us across miles of rocky terrain barren of trees and wildlife. A patchy layer of grass struggled to grow in the crushed shale and sandstone. We might have been driving across the Serengeti. All of the laughter from the back of the truck had ceased.

Under the 1977 Surface Mining Control and Reclamation Act, mountaintop mines must either be reclaimed to their "approximate original contour" (which never happens) or coal operators must obtain a variance showing they will convert the land to a "higher or better use." What this has come to mean, however, is that most operators simply do the cheapest thing—they seed the flattened site with some legume, often an exotic species, and call it "pasture" or "wildlife habitat."

Ben was quiet as we drove along; then he asked, "When are they going to reclaim this land?"

"It has been reclaimed," I said. "They sprayed hydroseed, so now this qualifies as wildlife habitat."

"This is it?"

"This is all the law requires."

Ben went quiet again. Finally he said, "This is obscene." I kept driving, the wheels kicking up dust. "I have to tell you," Ben said, "this is having an effect on me."

I could see that he was struggling to make his politics match up with what he was seeing, and nothing was making sense.

Finally Ben asked, "What do you think would happen if every University of Kentucky student came to see this?"

Because we teachers are often better at asking questions than answering them, I made the classic teacher move and turned the question back on Ben.

"I think something would have to change," he said.

I took no pleasure in Ben's painful epiphany. Aldo Leopold once wrote that "to receive an ecological education is to realize that we live in a world of wounds." I suspect that such an education began that day for Ben. But it might never have happened inside my classroom back at UK, where Ben could think of "the environment" as some vague realm that seemed to agitate left-leaning Americans like me. Indeed, one of the major obstacles facing environmental education is just that—the very term "environment" is far too abstract to elicit much real emotion from students, the kind of emotion that is necessary if we want them to translate information into knowledge and translate knowledge into responsible action. But learning through direct experience, direct perception, leads to different conclusions—conclusions like the one Ben reached as we drove across the strip mine.

Such learning, I think, is particularly important in the eastern coalfields of the United States precisely because those landscapes are under siege. A few summers ago, I conducted a writing workshop in Craftsbury Commons, Vermont. Because I had just finished a book about mountaintop-removal strip mining, I suggested as the title for my workshop, "Writing about Endangered Landscapes." Most of the members of my group came from New England states. Slowly, I realized that they seemed puzzled by my writing prompts. And finally I began to understand why: they didn't think of the places where they live *as* endangered. No one will ever blow the tops off the Green Mountains; even billboards are banned there because they represent "visual pollution." But as a Kentuckian, I have grown accustomed to thinking that the landscapes I love most could be clear-cut, the gorges flooded, the mountains annihilated with explosives, and the streams below those mountains buried under mining debris. And it is all perfectly legal, or at least permitted by regulatory agencies that look the other way. When I realized this profoundly different way of thinking about native landscapes, I began to understand how important Ben's question really was: "What if every UK student could see this?" For one thing, the question inevitably implies Ben's answer: something would have to change. And that answer implies another conclusion: the best way to save Robinson Forest is to make it possible for more students to come and experience the forest for themselves, to discover on their own why it might be *worth* saving. Yet on an even broader level, Ben's question suggests how significant experiential learning could be in this region for students of all ages and how important Robinson Forest could be as a laboratory where that learning might take place.

Unfortunately, a minuscule percentage of UK students, or students from Kentucky's primary schools, ever visit Robinson Forest or witness the strip mining that surrounds and threatens it. In fact, one of the arguments from the coal industry is that the forest itself should be strip-mined because UK has failed to carry out E. O. Robinson's mandate to educate students and the public in the functions of these vital watersheds. My response is that the university absolutely does need to do a better job of bringing people from across the state into these watersheds. Every weekend and during the week, Camp Robinson should be humming with 4-H clubs, Scouts, Governor's Scholar programs, church groups, and classes from every school and university in Kentucky. Given that Robinson Forest is one of the last and largest examples of the eastern mixed mesophytic forest, it represents a rare and vital place to engage in the kind of education that pushes well beyond the limitations of the standard curriculum. It is a place where students can actually read what Thoreau called nature's *hypaethral* text—the unroofed book. It is a text where words revert back into things and the walls of the classroom fall away.

The number of Americans who visit our national parks has dropped precipitously in recent years, and the allure of digital environments and electronic devices has a great deal to do with it. And yet, in an era of climate crisis, unsustainable resource consumption, and the sixth great extinction in the planet's history, American students need an ecological education more urgently than they ever have. Writer and teacher David Orr observed that too often in this country, education has served only to make Americans "better vandals"—affluent, uncritical consumers and exploiters of the natural world. My contention is that we can correct and redirect this trajectory, and we can instill in students an authentic concern for the natural world if we ground a new kind of curriculum in places like Robinson Forest.

It is there that the bland abstraction of environmentalism becomes the concrete particulars of moving water, enormous capstones, and flying squirrels. A century ago, America's foremost philosopher of education, John Dewey, put forward and tested the idea that education is best accomplished through an "intimate acquaintance with nature at first hand, with real things and materials." Such in situ experience, he came to believe, would result in transformative learning. Contemporary research has since confirmed that students retain 90 percent of what they learn if they learn by doing. Often when I am with my students in Robinson Forest, I feel that I am teaching them and reminding myself of one primary lesson: *pay attention.* Pay attention to your senses, to what you see, hear, smell, touch, and sometimes (in the case of wild greens) taste; pay attention to the way your mind registers what your body senses. Several decades of research at the University of Michigan has shown that the natural world actually restores human attention at a remarkable rate. Psychologist Stephen Kaplan called this attention restoration theory, or ART. Participants in one study who wandered through the university's arboretum performed far better on an attention test called the "backward digit-span task" than those who had walked through downtown Ann Arbor.

Back on UK's campus, students seem to pay scant attention to anything other than human-made or electronic environments. But when those fall away in the forest, students are suddenly confronted directly with the unmediated, largely unaltered natural world. Then the experience of seeing often gains a renewed clarity and intensity, and such close observation begins what I have come to understand as a three-step process of active learning: (1) see the thing, (2) engage the thing through representation, and (3) more fully understand the thing. Each of the steps tends to reinforce the others: to sketch a wild orchid, for instance, helps the artist to see it better. And representing a wild orchid through writing, drawing, or photography "intensifies the mutual interaction between the representation and the thing represented in the reader's mind," wrote Walter H. Clark Jr., cofounder of the New England Literature Program. The mind becomes a two-way mirror that reflects both the thing itself and the representation of that thing; and in both cases the mind more actively perceives both the orchid and, say, a poem about the orchid. Consider a beautiful poem by James Still, "I Was Born Humble":

I was born humble. At the foot of the mountains
My face was set upon the immensity of earth
And stone; and upon oaks full-bodied and old.
There is so much writ upon the parchment of leaves,
So much beauty blown upon the winds,
I can but fold my hands and sink my knees
In the leaf-pages. Under the mute trees
I have cried with this scattering of knowledge,
Beneath the flight of birds shaken with their waste
Of wings.
       I was born humble. My heart grieves
Beneath this wealth of wisdom perished with the leaves.

Reading this poem aloud with students at "the foot of the mountains," looking up at the chestnut oaks of Robinson Forest, is a much richer experience than reading it in a classroom. We can actually feel the wind in the poem and sink our own knees into the fallen "leaf-pages" that trouble the poet as he thinks of the wisdom that has "perished with the leaves."

Once, after a group of students and I had read "I Was Born Humble" in the forest, a student picked up an oak leaf, pointed to its network of veins, and said, "It looks like a map of this entire watershed and all of its streams." That, I thought, was an observation that would have pleased James Still, and it could only have come sitting under a chestnut oak and contemplating how "so much [is] writ on the parchment of leaves."

In addition to the more traditional form of representation that we most often associate with the humanities, I would add scientific field-work such as stream testing and data collection. When, for instance, Jim Krupa shows my nature writing class how to seine Clemons Fork for small fish that will indicate the stream's water quality, my students clearly gain knowledge that does not reside in a poem or a photograph or even the most beautiful page of Thoreau's journal. But what they learn wading in that cold water complements what they learned reading poetry while kneeling in the oak leaves. And just as Joyce Kilmer's famous poem "Trees" inspired North Carolinians to preserve the thirty-eight thousand old-growth acres that became the Joyce Kilmer Memorial Forest, so the information gathered in Clemons Fork—the information, for instance, that mining waste poses a grave threat to the survival of the stream's arrow darter—might lead to the preservation of Robinson Forest.

In the 1920s, the brilliant mathematician-philosopher Alfred North Whitehead warned that division and overspecialization within education would "produce minds in a groove" and ways of thinking inadequate "for the comprehension of human life." Whitehead emphasized that no body of knowledge, no one way of thinking, is superior to another. The well-educated student needs to understand a "variety of value"—different ways of seeing, measuring, and understanding the world and one's experience in it. "When you understand all about the sun and all about the atmosphere and all about the rotation of the earth, you may still miss the radiance of the sunset," Whitehead wrote in his classic book *Science and the Modern World*. If one is to fully experience an orange sunset, the atmospheric science that explains it must be accompanied by the aesthetic appreciation that intensifies it.

Whitehead, and many after him, blamed the rise of scientific materialism and philosophical dualism in the seventeenth century for creating both a scientific suspicion of the humanities and a dangerous divide between human culture and the natural world. John Locke typified this position when he wrote that "the intrinsic natural worth of anything consists in its fitness to supply the necessities or serve the conveniences of human life." The lingering effect of those divisions can be seen today in the coal industry's contempt for the mountains surrounding Robinson Forest—one more reason that the forest itself provides such a necessary redoubt in which to create an alternative curriculum. Such a curriculum would take the *watershed* as both its model and its metaphor, and thus it would seek to emulate some of the laws of an ecosystem: interdependence, diversity, and conservation. It would emphasize interdisciplinary learning through diverse subjects, a conservation ethic, and an emphasis on local knowledge. And it would try to break down many of the dualisms—grounded in Descartes' fundamental separation of mind and nature—that constrain traditional education in the United States.

Such a task actually began in 1837 when Ralph Waldo Emerson delivered the Phi Beta Kappa address at Harvard. In "An American Scholar" Emerson upended the traditional view that the role of philosophy was simply to "know thyself." Nature, Emerson claimed, was a mirror of the soul, "its laws the laws of [one's] own mind." Therefore, "the ancient precept, 'Know thyself,' and the modern precept, 'Study nature,' become at last one maxim." And with that, Emerson leapt nimbly across the great fissure Descartes had created between mind and nature. The American Pragmatists William James, John Dewey, and Jane Addams immediately understood what Emerson was up to and pushed to eliminate all distinctions between knowing and doing, asserting that any belief or piece of knowledge that did not elicit some action was of little consequence. And that too, I have noticed, is a principle that students in Robinson Forest often adopt. They take what they have learned back to UK's main campus and apply it in a number of actions, which have even included sit-ins at the UK president's office to protest logging in the forest.

The knowing-doing dichotomy, along with the disciplinary boundaries between the sciences and the humanities, are just two of the unhelpful dualisms that tend to break down in Robinson Forest. Divisions also disappear between teacher and students, class time and leisure time. In

Robinson Forest, the teacher is always learning alongside the students because the experience of being in the forest is always changing. A classroom on UK's main campus is always more or less the same classroom, but to paraphrase the poet A. R. Ammons, no walk in Robinson Forest is ever the same walk. One day you see bobcat tracks, the next you find elk scat, and the next you almost step on a copperhead. The teacher is often only one more set of eyes, and the students are no longer passive learners, empty vessels into which the teacher pours knowledge. In Robinson Forest, teaching and learning is a collaborative venture. When my eleventh-grade algebra teacher went home for the day, I just assumed that she etherized into a state of suspended animation until the next day's class. It never occurred to me that she had a life too. I think many American students feel this way about their teachers (in part because the culture as a whole thinks so poorly of its teachers). But in Robinson Forest there is no place for the teacher to disappear. I eat with my students and sit around the campfire with them and, I'll hazard to guess, become somewhat humanized in their minds.

Another reason the teacher-student hierarchy disappears is because the distinction between class time and out-of-class time gradually dissolves as my students and I spend time in the forest. A few years ago I met an Austrian professor who taught half the year in Vienna and half in the United States. I asked him to compare American and European college students. He said the main difference is that when American students leave class, they immediately start talking about last weekend's parties, upcoming parties, and other things that have no relation whatsoever to the class they just left. But when his Viennese students leave class, a group of them will inevitably find a café or bar and continue the discussion that began in class. And often the teacher is invited to go along, no longer *as* the teacher, but as someone with shared intellectual interests. In Robinson Forest I watch American students turn into, as it were, their European counterparts. Gradually, the entire forest becomes the classroom, and the whole day becomes the class discussion. What we do "in class," which is usually held outside anyway, becomes a directive for how to better inhabit the singular experience of being in the wild. And because the streams, hillsides, and capstones all seem pieces of Thoreau's unroofed book, it is hard, while in Robinson Forest, *not* to be in a classroom, just as it is inversely hard to feel that one *is* in a classroom.

As all of these dualisms dissipate, the learning that takes place in Robinson Forest begins to feel more integrated and more intuitive. Things I have to prod my students to do back on the main campus, like read poetry out loud, become after-dinner rituals in the forest as we relax on the large wooden porch of the main cabin. When the night falls early behind the steep ridgetops, the poetry reading often leads to playing acoustic music around a campfire. The fire pit pulls students toward it in the same way a large TV dominates the American family room. Except in the forest we entertain ourselves, usually with guitars, drums, and fiddles. This "un-plugged" nature of both the education and the entertainment is, I think, a crucial element of the students' Robinson Forest sojourn. It reveals to them the unexpected pleasures of an experience unmediated by electronic technology. Almost everything they see and touch, from their classmates to the maidenhair fern to their cabins and their musical instruments, is alive or was once alive. The two steep ridges that frame the narrow valley where Camp Robinson was built create a geographical intimacy that leads, in the course of a few days, to a tight sense of community among students and teacher. Moreover, that sense of solidarity extends beyond the humans to include the ridges themselves and the species that abide there. By walking everywhere we go—moving at the speed at which we naturally evolved to move—my students and I actually enact the fundamental ecological principle that says all organisms within a watershed are symbiotic parts of that larger whole. We feel, as a Jim Wayne Miller poem says, that "the mountains have come closer." We no longer suffer from the urban assumption that we humans are *over here* while "the environment" is *out there*. That dualism between nature and culture vanishes as well.

The Genesis creation story tell us that the first man, Adam, took his name from the Hebrew word for clay, *adamah*. And theologian Norman Wirzba pointed out that the words "human" and "humus" reflect this same strong connection between humans and the literal soil of the earth. To explore Robinson Forest—to examine, draw, photograph, or record in a journal the life that rises from that humus—is to expand on our definition of the self, to escape the flimsy narcissism that is constantly on sale to us in the city and suburb, and to understand again why Emerson said that to study nature *is* to study the self. It is to expand the definition of the subject to *include* the object, and to see that the object is actually another subject. The Japanese poet Basho once told his students that great poetry issues forth only when the poet and the natural world merge into a single understanding. This poetic principle is also an ecological principle—trees turn carbon dioxide into the oxygen that keeps us alive—and an ethical principle—the Golden Rule extended to include all of life. Biologist E. O. Wilson put this more expansive understanding of who we are beautifully: "Humanity is exalted not because we are so far above other living creatures, but because knowing them well elevates the very concept of life." It elevates the concept of life because it turns knowledge into empathy, and empathy becomes the beginning of the actions we take to preserve the concept of life—to preserve, for instance, the mountains of southern Appalachia.

Along with the "humus-human" connection, Norman Wirzba also called our attention back to the fact that the word "culture" derives from the Latin *cultus*, meaning "to cultivate and care for the land." Yet there is almost nothing in American popular culture that reflects this original connection between nature and culture. In film and on TV, those who work the land are usually held up for ridicule as ignorant rubes from a bygone day. In truck commercials, a mountainous landscape is only something to be conquered by rugged men in four-wheel drives. And the sorry nonsense we hear today on country radio stations has no connection at all to the Tulare dust or the California cotton fields that Merle Haggard once wrote and sang about. In fact, Toby Keith's hit "American Ride" doesn't so much deny global warming as revel in it:

> That's us, that's right,
> Gotta love this American ride.
> Both ends of the ozone burnin',
> Funny how the world keeps turnin'.

American popular culture and consumer culture have become so intertwined, so mutually reinforcing, that those commercial forces have become directly linked to the ruination of our soil, air, and water.

I am not going to claim that taking students to places like Robinson Forest will "cure" them of their addiction to popular culture and the technology that disseminates it, nor do I think that would be an entirely good idea. But I do think moving the classroom to the forest (where there is no cell phone reception) gives students an opportunity to rediscover and reestablish that crucial, original connection between nature and culture, *adam* and *adamah*. That can mean redefining the term "culture" in ways that reclaim lost regional traditions. When the people of Appalachia invented country music, for example, they weren't thinking about sold-out concerts and tour buses. Indeed, they weren't thinking about an *audience* at all. More often than not, they were simply family members collaborating with a few different instruments to entertain themselves and perhaps their neighbors. Such music bound members of a community together because they shared the same songs, and often their version of that song differed considerably from the version played one hollow over. I think that sense of cultural solidarity grounded in a particular place is worth reviving, especially in an age of increasing transience and homogenized urban and suburban landscapes. I also think that students, by creating artifacts out of their experiences in Robinson Forest, can find varied and interesting ways to bridge the divide between nature and culture. They begin to see how the natural world can sustain a rich culture, just as that culture can go a long way toward preserving and building sustainable environments.

A watershed, after all, is not simply a natural landscape; it is also a storied landscape, and those stories are inextricably bound to the land where they were born. By weaving the stories of the eastern mountains, the stories of the coalfields, into the natural history of Robinson Forest, we build a richly layered curriculum in the same way the forest builds topsoil. Some of the most fascinating chapters of American history were written right here at the headwaters of the Kentucky River watershed, often in blood. Here Aunt Molly Jackson (the "Pistol Packin' Mama") held up a coal company store and stole flour to feed starving children in a coal camp. Here, in a house surrounded by coal company gun thugs, Florence Reece pulled a page from a wall calendar and wrote down what would become the world's most famous union song, "Which Side Are

You On?" Here miners fought and died until "Bloody" Harlan County became the last county in the United States to earn the right to collective bargaining. And it was here that the widow Ollie Combs became an instant folk hero by sitting down in front of a bulldozer that was about to flatten her home in order to extract the minerals beneath it.

This is important history that tells us much about the effects of industrialism on a rural culture and about the power struggles that have made modern Appalachia such a hard-worn and complicated place. Furthermore, these are lessons that can be compared and applied around the world—in Nigeria, for instance, where a similar combination of rich resources and poor people has had similar crushing effects. But my point here is that local knowledge and a local curriculum are particularly important for students from Kentucky and from the southern Appalachian Mountains. In the first place, when students read about the places they are from, particularly in books by native writers, they begin to feel their own home legitimated, validated. "When I was growing up in these mountains," wrote Kentucky novelist Lee Smith, "I was always taught that culture was someplace else, and that when the time came, I'd be sent off to get some. Now everybody here realizes that we don't have to go anyplace to 'get culture'—we've got our own, and we've had it all along." In fact, it was actually seeing the name of her own hometown, Grundy, Kentucky, in James Still's novel *River of Earth* that inspired the young Lee Smith to become a writer.

Localizing knowledge makes the curriculum more relevant to students' own experience, and it can instill a sense of pride about the places where our students live. Such pride can lead to a desire to take responsibility for those places, just as such taking of responsibility can lead to a feeling of pride. By focusing on local issues, what we might call the "watershed curriculum" can also develop a progressive, problem-solving impulse. And a curriculum geared more toward addressing local problems can begin to reflect the overall sense of purpose that best drives and unites all disciplines. Furthermore, because most of the problems that students identify within and around the watersheds of Robinson Forest cannot be solved by one discipline alone, an opportunity arises for students to see the complementary nature of different fields of study. Such learning is inevitably interdisciplinary because real problems, and real learning, rarely break down along clear disciplinary lines. If a strip mine on the outskirts of Robinson Forest is polluting Buckhorn Creek, that is clearly a biological and chemical problem, but it is also an ethical problem grounded in lessons of history. To solve it, many fields of knowledge must be brought to bear. And to articulate the solution will require skilled rhetoric indeed. Working to solve that problem becomes an experiment in stewardship—the opposite of what David Orr called education-as-vandalism. It also brings us back to the Pragmatists' idea that when education is at its best, learning and doing are indistinguishable. In this sense, John Dewey's definition of philosophy can just as easily be understood as a definition of education: "an outlook upon future possibilities with reference to attaining the better and averting the worse." The "worse" can be plainly seen on the strip mines that surround Robinson Forest. Yet the forest itself represents both a model and a proving ground for the "better"—better land use and a better, more sustainable form of education.

ROBINSON FOREST

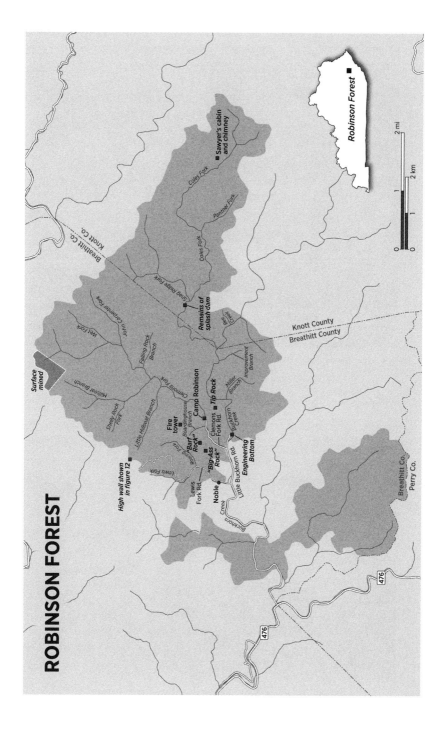

Robinson Forest

Surface mined

Knott Co.
Breathitt Co.

High wall shown in figure 12

Sawyer's cabin and chimney

Coles Fork

Panther Fork

Coles Fork

Snag Ridge Fork

Remains of splash dam

Knott County
Breathitt County

West Fork

John Carpenter Fork

Falling Rock Branch

Millseat Branch

Clemons Fork

Camp Robinson

Tip Rock

Miller Branch

Improvement Branch

Shelly Rock Fork

Little Millseat Branch

Fire tower

Boardinghouse Branch

"Barf Rock"

Clemons Fork Rd.

Buckhorn Rd.

Buckhorn Creek

Guy Cole Branch

"Big-Ass Rock"

Lewis Fork Rd.

Noble

Little Buckhorn Rd.

Engineering Bottom

Lewis Fork

Buckhorn Creek

Breathitt Co.
Perry Co.

476

476

2 mi

2 km

Splash dam similar to those constructed along Coles Fork before 1912.
(Special Collections & Archives, Hutchins Library, Berea College)

Sawmill at unknown location in Robinson Forest, perhaps at
Camp Robinson or in Engineering Bottom on Buckhorn Creek.
(University of Kentucky Archives)

Timber Estimates
Robinson Forest

Species	Cords	Board Ft
Beech	14,047	816,480
Chestnut	12,887	1,621,640
Hickory	5,542	1,180,360
Black Walnut	81	28,360
White Oak	2,007	945,310
Chestnut Oak	3,160	1,527,740
Red Oak	632	396,860
Black Oak	2,618	892,410
Scarlet Oak	4,441	960,860
Hard Maple	579	106,830
Red Maple	2,588	167,880
Yellow Poplar	766	810,230
Cucumber	585	159,410
Basswood	377	192,660
Black Gum	4,121	333,970
Ash	212	52,290
Shortleaf Pine	279	306,940
Pitch Pine	1,195	791,420
Hemlock	334	361,220
Birch	747	95,120
Miscellaneous	1,038	39,810
Dogwood	368	— —
Locust	57	— —
Total	58,661	11,787,800
Per Acre	4.5	1,175

Chestnut Oak bark 2,333 Cords
Locust Posts 8,851

Acres - Forest 13,263
Acres - Open 504

Date of Estimate - 1929

Original 1929 timber estimates for Robinson Forest. Although the chestnut blight reached Kentucky in 1924, the American chestnut was still extremely abundant in the forest, as indicated by the estimated board feet for that species. (Photo by James J. Krupa)

Sign that formerly stood at the entrance to Camp Robinson on Clemons Fork. (Photo by James J. Krupa)

Fire tower that stands on a ridgetop above Camp Robinson. This photo is from 1992, before southern bark beetles destroyed the larger pitch pines surrounding the tower's base. (Photo by James J. Krupa)

Two of the cabins in Camp Robinson as they looked in 1992. The cabins were built in the early 1950s with wood from American chestnuts killed by the blight. (Photo by James J. Krupa)

Characteristic rock shelter within a sandstone outcrop. Dormant brown rock tripe covers the sandstone. (Photo by James J. Krupa)

Charred forest floor above Lewis Fork Road after the November 2001 fire.
(Photo by James J. Krupa)

Mountaintop-removal strip mine like those that nearly surround Robinson Forest. The human-made culverts are "reconstructed mountain streams" constructed by the coal industry to satisfy post-mining reclamation rules. Active mining is visible in the center background. (Photo by James J. Krupa)

Typical outcrop in which woodrats reside. Weathering and erosion have left sandstone blocks stacked atop the outcrop. (Photo by James J. Krupa)

Tip Rock, on a ridgetop above Camp Robinson. The distinct layers are sedimentary deposits from ancient streams. (Photo by James J. Krupa)

Northern boundary of Robinson Forest. The forest edge rests on
a high wall resulting from mountaintop removal. The Surface Mine Control and
Reclamation Act of 1977 supposedly made high walls such as this one illegal.
(Photo by James J. Krupa)

Typical second-growth forest on lower slopes of Robinson Forest. The two larger
trunks are yellow poplars. (Photo by James J. Krupa)

Sandstone chimney near the top of Coles Fork is all that remains of a cabin in which one of Mowbray and Robinson's sawyers lived. (Photo by James J. Krupa)

Sunrise in Robinson Forest as viewed from the fire tower. Morning fog often fills the hollows, giving the impression from Camp Robinson that it is an overcast day, but it usually burns off by midmorning. (Photo by James J. Krupa)

Chestnut oak growing out from fractures in an outcrop. (Photo by James J. Krupa)

Buckhorn Creek in mid-spring. An exposed seam of sandstone borders the stream, with a stand of eastern hemlocks in the background. (Photo by James J. Krupa)

Fires in Robinson Forest, by year

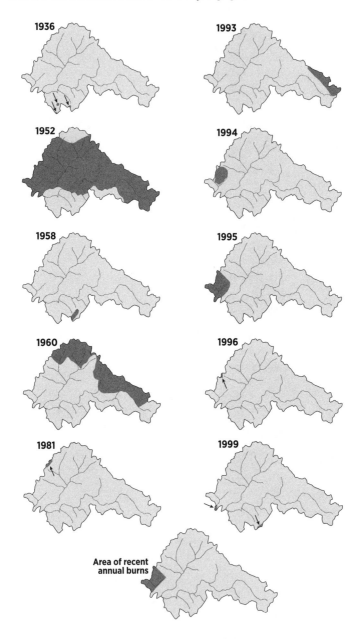

1936

1993

1952

1994

1958

1995

1960

1996

1981

1999

Area of recent
annual burns

The fire history of the main block of Robinson Forest as described by
Will and Junior Marshall. This map is all that remains of the Marshall family
oral history of Robinson's fires.

CHAPTER 4

Slumps and Slides and Steep, Steep Slopes

James J. Krupa

To truly experience Robinson Forest requires complete immersion in the woods away from roads and buildings, but few who visit the forest have the time or the opportunity to do that. Most visitors view the tall, steep slopes that define Robinson Forest from the comfort of Camp Robinson, or perhaps hike the path to the fire tower for a deeper experience. Labored breathing and sweat make it clear that these slopes are steep and tall. And yet this hike is a very mild dose of the challenges Robinson's slopes can offer. You must get off the path to understand that. Climbing the slopes off trail means slipping and falling, sweating and bleeding, accumulating cuts and scrapes, tripping over branches and rocks, getting dirt in your shoes and mud on your knees and on the seat of your pants. That is full immersion. I did not become connected to the forest until I got off the trails. I did not appreciate the slopes until I had aching knees and sore ankles, burning lungs and short breath. Climbing a slope is a dirty, sweaty, and sometimes painful experience. It is also a joyous, exuberant experience that ends with a sense of accomplishment on reaching the ridgetop.

To climb a slope sensibly, you ascend slowly, angling right and then left as though following a switchback trail. This is the smart way up; it reduces the steepness of the ascent, and I advise others to climb this way, especially first-timers. When I am with my students, I ignore my own advice and go straight up to get to the top as quickly as possible.

Ascending slopes that way is an adventure as well as an intense cardio-vascular workout. The faster I try to scramble up, the harder gravity pulls me back. When I first started running up Robinson's slopes, I was in good physical condition (and much younger), and yet each ascent made me feel badly out of shape. Even those who are agile and coordinated are shocked by how clumsy and ungraceful they become on the slopes. That is the nature of Robinson's slopes: they create self-doubt.

When I take my classes to the forest on weekends, scrambling up slopes is a game. I go up as fast as I can for no other reason than to challenge myself, shock the students, and have fun. Shocking students is fun. When they stand in Camp Robinson looking up at the three ridges surrounding the camp, my students are viewing some of the tallest, steepest slopes in the forest. They are awestruck by how sharply the forest juts up into the sky. When I tell them we are going to climb the slopes, some students are excited; others are apprehensive if not downright appalled. They may find it pointless and absurd to climb something so steep, but climb it we do.

The slopes in Robinson Forest range in height from two hundred feet to six hundred feet. The least challenging slopes ascend at a thirty-five-degree angle. The most punishing has a seventy-degree rise. No two slopes are alike. Often the steepest part of the climb is just below the ridgetop. Steep angles often end in a flat, horizontal surface known as a bench. Benches meander across slopes like contour lines on a topographic map. They can be as wide as a two-lane road, and indeed, some were used as logging roads in the past. Some slopes have as many as three benches, like giant steps leading to the ridgetop; others have two or just one, and a few have none.

Slopes, like outcrops, are shaped by wind and rain, freezing and thawing, expansion and contraction. Subject to gravity, they are also shaped by the geological events of slumping, creep, and sliding. Slumping is a large-scale event that can span the length of a slope. Like creep, it is a slow process that takes place over a long period. When slumping occurs, a large swath of the forested slope slides downhill. Fractured seams of sandstone can pull apart, leaving exposed vertical surfaces of rock up to twenty feet thick protruding from a slope. The large dislodged blocks of sandstone below an exposed seam look like giant pieces of a jigsaw puzzle. Slumping has given Robinson Forest much of its shape and character. Creep occurs on a smaller scale and is best exemplified by the rocks, blocks, and boulders scattered along the slopes. Each is on a slow journey downhill, headed toward the stream below. Inch by inch over the millennia, these pieces of sandstone slowly creep down the slope.

The only cave known to exist in Robinson Forest was exposed by slumping and represents one of best examples of this geological phenomenon in the forest. The slope on which it is found has a long, horizontal ditch that is lined above and below with large pieces of sandstone. On the uphill side, a sandstone seam protrudes. The ditch is the demarcation line between stable soil above and slumping, unstable soil below. The inconspicuous mouth of the cave is located just above the ditch at the base of another exposed seam of sandstone. The exposed rock has a series of fractures that have widened to crevices. Cold air flows out from some of these, suggesting they are probably connected to a hidden cave system. The exposed cave has a large chamber and a series of vertical and horizontal crevices, some wide enough for a person to walk through. Allegheny woodrats live in the cave, as does the only maternal colony of Rafinesque's big-eared bats in the forest. More than one hundred bats give birth and raise their young there. The big-eared is the most impressive of the bats in Robinson Forest: its large body is covered with long, smoky gray fur, and its inch-long ears curl back like ram's horns when the bat is at rest. It is doubtful that big-eared bats would exist in Robinson if slumping had not provided them with a home.

Slides, the third of the geological events that shape slopes, are occasional and isolated. They can occur where a hot fire has swept across a slope, killing trees whose roots had held soil in place. Heavy rains play a role as well; they soak and saturate the organic-rich topsoil but are unable to penetrate the impermeable mineral soil below. Water flowing downhill over the mineral soil creates a slippery, fluid plane, and the topsoil above destabilizes and gives way. More frequently, slides are the result of human activity. A road cut destabilizes a slope; removing trees above the road causes further destabilization. A heavy downpour can trigger a slide that may bury roads, benches, and streams in a moment.

Over the course of fifteen years, nearly seven hundred students have followed me up the slopes of Robinson Forest. I entice them with the promise of live-trapping woodrats and flying squirrels. To ease them in on the first day, we climb the south-facing slope below the ridgetop on which Johnson Rock, Big Ass Rock, and Barf Rock rest. It is a slope that starts off at forty-five degrees and ends with a sixty-degree rise just below the ridgetop. The hardier students carry super-sized backpacks holding metal cage traps and bait such as apples and balls of peanut butter mixed with oatmeal. The five strongest and most fit carry packs loaded with forty pounds of peanut butter–soaked dog food, which will distract raccoons from harassing the traps. A raccoon stuffed with dog food and peanut butter is less inclined to pull traps out of trees or from rock crevices. In short, we haul up a lot of mass.

We climb slowly, stopping at each bench to catch our breath and set traps, placing the final set of traps along the ridgetop. This first climb eases everyone into the routine. The experience is an unexpected shock for most first-timers, who will likely have aching muscles by the end of the day. Few complain on the first day; they feel victorious after successfully ascending a slope. Bright and early the next morning, we head back up to collect our traps. Any sense of victory from the day before is soon crushed. We gather at the base of the east-facing slope directly below Barf Rock. I point up the slippery sixty-degree rise, telling them that Barf Rock, six hundred feet above, rests at the end of a ridgeline. It is hidden by the dense forest, but I assure them it is up there.

I caution them to take their time and move at their own pace, and promise to wait for them at the top. Then I take off up the slope at my fastest pace. The most athletic students shoot past me, racing each other to be the first to reach Barf Rock. Most other students labor on their way up this much more difficult climb, spreading out in a line of bodies snaking up the slope. My teaching assistant is assigned the task staying at the end of the line in case a student is having trouble. My goal is to get to the top as fast as I can so that I can sit on Barf Rock, relax, catch my breath, and let my legs dangle over the edge while I watch the others ascend. For some, the origin of the name Bark Rock becomes apparent. Students who stayed up too late last night, consumed too much contraband alcohol, or had too much breakfast pay the price.

Several years ago, as we were preparing to begin the morning ascent, a student named Lonnie ate an enormous breakfast to prepare himself for a rigorous day in the forest. For reasons I still don't understand, Lonnie decided that twelve chocolate pancakes smothered in chocolate syrup was the breakfast he needed. Lonnie was the last to reach Barf Rock; the pancakes didn't make it to the top.

The students sprawled at Barf Rock after the climb are a sight. Sweat-soaked and red-faced, some lean against trees and guzzle water. Others sprawl over flat sandstone slabs, breathing hard. All of them are elated by their accomplishment. Many a group photo has been taken at this outcrop to mark the occasion: a group of victorious students now deeply immersed in Robinson Forest, seeing and feeling its rugged beauty.

I have another attitude toward the slopes when I am by myself in Robinson Forest, doing research. No silliness, no trying to scramble up the slopes as fast as possible. Research time is all about conserving my energy and getting the most out of my legs before they are spent. I climb up and down the slopes and hike ridgetops from sunrise to sunset, covering as much ground and accomplishing as much as possible before exhaustion consumes me. I climb with my knees bent and my back parallel to the ground to lower my center of gravity and reduce the risk of a hard fall; I keep at least three points of contact with the ground. Falling with a heavy backpack loaded with equipment will have serious consequences—damaging the equipment, hurting me enough to end my work, or both. I climb the slopes at a steady, moderate pace. I grab rocks and saplings, using arm strength to pull me up, saving my leg muscles.

I have spent cold, snowy December days climbing Robinson's slopes. I have spent hot, humid July days doing the same. Three consecutive days of climbing slopes is all I can take. The first day is exhilarating: legs working like pistons, lungs on fire, heart pounding, my clothes soaked with sweat. The first night all my muscles are tight and fatigued, but I sleep well. Into the second day, my legs cramp and my body aches. My pace slows. My arms are scratched raw by thorny tangles of greenbriers. Sleeping is difficult the second night. My muscles are knotted and throbbing. They burn all night. By the third day, every slope is a struggle. My climbing is labored and slow, my enthusiasm is gone, and I am exhausted. Day three ends early. My body simply needs to recover. I have never felt as much a part of Robinson Forest as I do after three days of climbing slopes. I have climbed them all, most more than once.

The steep slopes of Robinson Forest are among the factors responsible for the tremendous tree diversity. Temperatures and moisture levels vary from top to bottom, creating many microclimates; they range from hot and dry on the high slopes to cool and wet at the base of the slopes. In addition, the microclimate of a north-facing slope is distinctly different from that of a warmer, drier south-facing slope. Different species of trees have different ideal growing conditions. Species that thrive in the cool, wet hollows and on north-facing slopes rarely grow on ridgetops and south-facing slopes. The incredible diversity of Robinson's trees gradually unfolds to someone slowly descending one of Robinson's slopes, moving from drier to moister soil along the way. Transitions from one tree community to the next become obvious as species abundant on upper slopes disappear and others come to dominate the lower reaches.

The ridgetops and high slopes are where oaks and pines thrive. Chestnut oaks, scarlet oaks, pitch pines, and short-leaf pines dominate, with Virginia pines scattered about. Hickories, black gums, and red maples are abundant. Thickets of small blueberry bushes fill sunlit patches of forest floor below gaps in the canopy. This is the driest, warmest, windiest part of the slope, and the plants that thrive here are those best adapted for these conditions. Floating blocks of sandstone litter the high slopes, just beginning their journey downward, creeping inch by inch past oaks and pines. The blocks are large and solid and face a future of constant attack by the forces of nature.

To someone visiting for a day or once every few months, Robinson Forest's ecology seems unchanging. Yet, change is evident to those who have spent years in the forest. In 2000, the high slopes lost most of their stands of pines. Southern bark beetles pulsed up from the Southeast into Robinson Forest that year, with pitch pines and short-leaf pines hit the hardest, and Virginia pines hit the least. The attack happened quickly, and by the time we realized the beetle was in the forest, the damage was done. In November 2000 I took a photo from the fire tower showing the tall, lush pines that surrounded it. When I returned in February 2001, I was shocked to see every one of these pines dead and brown. The beetles had been chewing their way through the cambium of the trees since sometime late in 2000. Pine needles can remain green for weeks after the tree is dead, and no one realized at the time what was happening.

In the months that followed, dead brown needles blanketed the ground. Then large slabs of pine bark peeled free and crashed down on top of the beds of needles, revealing naked trees crisscrossed with tunnels left by the beetles as they chewed through the cambium. Within a few years, dead pines were collapsing everywhere. Once-thriving stands of pines lay like giant matchsticks on the ground. Having exhausted their food supply, the beetle population crashed and the species retreated back south. Fortunately, many pine seedlings survived, and seeds safely hidden in the forest floor began to sprout. Many seedlings have sprung up; some are now four feet tall. In time, perhaps, pines will once again be among the dominant trees on the ridgetops and high slopes.

Benches along the high slopes often rest atop expansive seams of sandstone exposed by erosion. Sandstone acts as an impermeable layer preventing water from escaping, and the benches on the high, dry slopes can be surprisingly wet. Plants that prefer the cool, moist hollows far below occasionally grow on wet benches, American beech, hemlocks, wild hydrangea, pawpaw, rosebay rhododendron, and black willow among them. The benches have shallow pools that remain filled much of the year and dry up only during the hottest, driest summer months.

Temporary bench pools have an important ecological role in Robinson Forest. Without them, most of Robinson's amphibians would be able to breed only at the base of the slopes in pools adjacent to streams, and few amphibians would live in the higher elevations. Many salamanders, frogs, and toads need shallow, temporary pools to lay their eggs. Decomposing leaves and the associated microbial life that feeds on them provide nutrients and food for amphibian larvae. Predators requiring permanent water, such as leeches and predaceous diving beetles, cannot survive in temporary bench pools. Tadpoles and salamander larvae in the pools have few predators, but they must compete with each other for the limited food. They race with time and with each other to grow, metamorphose, and escape the pool before it evaporates.

Bench pools come to life in early February. Male wood frogs with raccoon-like masks arrive in swarms and swim about over the pool's surface calling for mates. The males remain in the pools during most of the short breeding season; females stay only a few hours to mate and lay their eggs. This skews the nightly sex ratio to three or more males for every female and forces the males into intense competition for mates. A successful male rides the back of his mate in a position called amplexus. Holding his belly tight against the female's back, he buries his fists in her armpits and holds on as other males attempt to dislodge him. The female releases eggs from her cloaca as the male releases sperm from his. The eggs and sperm mix together and float to the surface, forming a mat with contributions from many pairs. After releasing her eggs, the female leaves the pool and disappears into the leaf litter. The male remains and searches for other females. Many males fail to mate; others mate often—either by luck or because they possess some attribute that gives them a competitive edge. Successful males might be stronger, and thus better able to grasp a female or to pry other amplecting males free from their mate; or they might have a call more attractive to females. In the end, some males will win the mating contest, siring more tadpoles than their competitors. After a few weeks, the chaotic, cacophonous orgy grows silent as the wood frogs drift away into the forest floor, leaving behind developing eggs and hatching tadpoles.

A succession of amphibian species uses the bench pools as spring progresses, each with its own mating ritual. Yellow-spotted salamanders arrive on the heels of the departing wood frogs. These chubby, slow-moving amphibians are strikingly colored with large yellow blotches scattered over shiny blue-black skin. Secretive and nocturnal, they look like eight-inch-long rubber toys. Female yellow-spotted salamanders lay dense, round, gelatinous balls of eggs that often appear green from the algae growing within. On one trip to the forest, I was showing a group of students the masses of eggs, letting them pick one up to hold and pass around before placing it back in the pool. One person exclaimed that they have the firmness, feel, size, and shape of silicone breast implants. That image comes to mind now whenever I find salamander egg masses floating in pools.

Along with spotted salamanders come spring peepers: tiny, delicate frogs that gather around the pool's edge and in nearby trees and shrubs. Spring peepers fill the forest with their melodious calls, yet are so small and so secretive that they are rarely seen. The peepers depart and are replaced by their equally small relatives the mountain chorus frogs, which produce a call that sounds like a thumb rubbed across the teeth of a comb. The amorous little males call night and day with only their heads exposed above the water's surface. When danger approaches, they stop calling and remain motionless, camouflaged by their green-and-gray-striped bodies. If the threat continues, they slowly sink to the bottom of the pool, hide beneath rotting leaves, and wait for the danger to pass. Chorus frogs are miniature ventriloquists. It is next to impossible for one person to pinpoint a calling male because the call always seems to reso-nate from somewhere else in the pool. To see chorus frogs in the act of calling requires two people triangulating toward the sound. I have stood in the dark with a student a few feet away, flashlights ready but turned off. When a male begins to call, we simultaneously flick on our lights, pointing toward what we perceive as the source. Usually the beams of light strike the water a few feet apart. We step closer together and nearer to the sound, turn off our lights, and wait. When the male resumes call-ing, we direct our lights toward the sound source again. Eventually, both beams of light will fall on the calling chorus frog. As long as we remain motionless and quiet, the tiny male will continue to call, oblivious to the light. It is amazing that such a tiny creature can produce such a loud sound.

As spring advances and nights warm, American toads arrive and fill the night with their melodious trills. Each male stakes out a claim along the edge of the pool and begins to call for a mate. They make little effort to hide and are easily watched. Male American toads behave with rela-tive civility when their numbers are low, but when large male congrega-tions form, chaos ensues. Calling males scramble madly about in search of females. Females, far outnumbered by males, stealthily select a suit-able mate while avoiding detection by the other males. Once mated, the pair may stay together for twenty-four hours. They hide in a clump of debris and wait for daylight, when unsuccessful males will leave the pool.

Swarms of unmated males are a threat to the mated pair, with some trying to pry the two apart while others try to amplex the female. The confusion grows as males grab other males, ignoring their release calls (the polite way for a male to indicate that another male has made an incorrect choice). A ball of amorous toads forms, often trapping the mated pair inside. More males pile on. The helpless pair is forced underwater, where, unable to escape, they drown. Mating and laying eggs can be a deadly business; avoiding detection is crucial. By late spring the toads are gone and gray tree frogs arrive at the bench pools to enact their own mating ritual.

As breeding amphibians come and go, pools fill with eggs, salamander larvae, and tadpoles. Some pools contain only a few tadpoles of a single species. Other pools have hundreds, perhaps even thousands of larvae and tadpoles of many species. Competition for food is intense as larval amphibians scramble to eat enough algae and leaf litter. The more they eat, the faster they grow. The faster they grow, the sooner they metamorphose, allowing them to leave the pool before it evaporates. Those that grow too slowly end up as part of the black crust at the bottom of a dry pool. In a wet year, many survivors emerge from bench pools, pouring out over the forest floor in waves to face a new set of dangers. In a dry year, few survive to leave the pool.

Continuing down the slope, pines, chestnut oaks, and scarlet oaks become less common while white oaks, black oaks, southern red oaks, pignut hickories, and mockernut hickories become more abundant. Black gums and maples persist. The magnificence of the tall, straight trees that dominate the lower slopes becomes apparent, particularly on the cooler, wetter north-facing slopes where massive shagbark hickories tower overhead.

I have spent many moments over the years relaxing on a bed of dried leaves on the forest floor, my back against a hickory, looking up at the forest canopy. Slender rays of sunlight penetrate the canopy here and there, occasionally reaching the ground. The understory is stippled with filtered light. I find it peaceful and serene. For trees, however, this is a battleground where a Darwinian struggle for existence plays out at an incredibly slow pace by humans' sense of time. Trees are engaged in a high-stakes battle for sunlight. Those that win capture the most sunlight and reap the rewards of greater growth and reproduction. Those that lose are buried under the canopy and struggle to photosynthesize enough food to survive. The tall, straight trees of Robinson Forest are evidence of the struggle. In a forest, the goal of capturing as much sunlight as possible is best accomplished by growing up, not out, by striving to be taller than competitors. In a city park or open field where trees are not crowded, a tree can grow both up and out to maximize the amount of sunlight captured, since there is little competition for light. In a forest, growing out is usually a losing strategy, although I have found massive chestnut oaks as wide as they are tall. Usually they were growing next to large outcrops. These are called wolf trees or lone wolf trees, and they tell a story. "Wolf tree" does not refer to a species, but to a shape that is a response to an environment free of competition. They are trees that survived a significant disturbance event such as logging or fire. With the surrounding trees gone, they were freed from competition and able to grow both up and out, taking on the very shape that defines a wolf tree. Eventually the forest filled in around these giants, which retain their impressive form. Wolf trees are much older than the adjacent trees. When I see a wolf tree next to an outcrop, I know it survived either a fire decades earlier or possibly the saws of Mowbray and Robinson's loggers.

A thick canopy blocks most sunlight from reaching the forest floor. Species such as sugar maple, holly, pawpaw, beech, and the magnolias do well in the shady understory, but do better when a gap opens in the canopy. Others, such as the oaks, are canopy trees that struggle to survive in the understory. Oak seedlings and saplings grow slowly in the understory, struggling in the shade to make enough food. These young trees are small and misshapen. Their best hope for survival is a catastrophic event that topples one of the giant canopy trees. Occasionally that happens. Windstorms can knock over the tallest trees. A heavy rain might loosen the thin layer of topsoil, weakening a tree's grip and sending it over. Age, disease, and decay can cause a trunk to rot even though the tree is still alive. Eventually the weakened trunk will buckle under the weight of the living branches and crash to the ground. Any of these scenarios will produce a gaping hole in the canopy. A flood of sunlight rushes in, spilling over the forest floor, and saplings and seedlings capture the light and begin to grow rapidly, racing to reach the gap above.

Some of the tiny oaks under the canopy are surprisingly old, perhaps twenty years. They have gnarled, bent, and dead branches and appear to be barely clinging to life, but in fact they have invested much of their energy in growing extensive, well-established root systems. Some forest ecologists refer to these as accumulators; that is, they accumulate in the understory beneath the canopy, waiting for a gap to form. If a gap does occur, the accumulator is ready, able to grow much faster than younger trees with smaller root systems. The accumulator reaching the gap first wins the race to become the next canopy tree. Terry Cunningham, manager of Pioneer Forest in the Ozarks of Missouri, calls these "smoldering oaks," likening them to smoldering embers under leaf litter that persist unnoticed for days after a fire and then explode into flame when the conditions are right.

Other species, such as the bigleaf magnolia, are masterful "gap seekers." They are understory trees that rarely become part of the canopy, but when an opening occurs, they respond, growing toward the brightest light in the canopy. As the patches of light shift from point to point over the years, the tree bends toward the shifting sunshine.

Like the tree communities near the ridgetops, the oaks and hickories that dominate the slopes are dynamic and ever changing. White oaks, which are common here, are ecologically versatile and commercially important, used for building ships, making furniture, and other kinds of construction. White oak is the only wood used for bourbon barrels. Ecological studies indicate that white oaks are in decline in many forests while red maple numbers are on the rise; the cause of this shift from oak to maple is a point of discussion and debate. The rise and fall in abundance of forest tree species has occurred as long as forests have existed, although human activities have made these fluctuations more rapid, extensive, and severe.

Fire, for example, can affect the relative dominance of tree species and has been present in Robinson Forest for as long as humans have been present to set them—and probably as long as there have been forests. Information gained from Cliff Palace Pond, an archaeological site a few miles north of Robinson Forest on the Cumberland Plateau, gives a hint of what Robinson's last 10,000 years may have been like. Charcoal deposits in lake and bog sediments show that fires were frequent from 9,500 to 7,500 years ago, from 6,500 to 4,500 years ago, and again over the last 3,000 years. Tree pollen preserved in these same sediments shows that fire-tolerant trees such as oaks and pines thrived during these periods while junipers suffered. In the absence of fire, maples and junipers thrived while oaks and pines declined.

We know with certainty that more than 80 percent of Robinson Forest has burned since it was given in trust to the University of Kentucky in 1923. Based on the Robinson Forest Inventory compiled by the forest's assistant superintendent (and later superintendent) John Overstreet and published in 1984, we also know that humans started all of the fires, and that most were deliberate acts of arson.

The first record of arson in the forest dates back to 1925. Robinson Forest was heavily settled when it became the property of the University of Kentucky. There was a homestead at the mouth of virtually every stream. In 1924 UK declared these inhabitants squatters and served them eviction notices. The abandoned dwellings were torn down and burned. Those evicted responded in kind with fire. Arson claimed two thousand acres from 1925 to 1926, and another twenty-six hundred acres from 1926 to 1930. UK responded by establishing a fire prevention and suppression policy. Beginning in 1930, firebreaks were dug along the forest boundary and local laborers were hired to fight fires in the forest. But this practice had unintended consequences. Because firefighting was the only source of income for many, some of the hired men started fires to generate work. UK was forced to discontinue the practice and instead relied on university staff stationed at Robinson Forest to fight fires.

The best record of the recent fire history of Robinson Forest resided in the memories of two men with a long connection to the region, Andrew "Junior" Marshall and his son Will. Three generations of Marshalls have worked for UK at Robinson Forest, beginning with Junior's father, Andrew B. Marshall, and the Marshall family history extends back more than two hundred years in the hollows of Breathitt County. The Marshalls' oral history of the region was deep and detailed, and for years

I felt an urgent need to record Junior's and Will's knowledge of Robinson Forest's fire history before their recollections were lost to time.

In 2001 I was preparing a manuscript on the mammals of Robinson Forest and their ecology. Because fires influence the ecology of a region's mammals, I wanted to include the Marshalls' knowledge in the study. I spent an August afternoon with Junior and Will retracing the paths of past fires on a three-foot-by-four-foot map of the forest.

I always looked forward to my chats with Will. He would fill me in on local gossip and politics, and on university politics dealing with the forest as well. He would tell me about the condition of the jeep trails—where trees might be down on the roads or if any recent slides had buried them. When I was studying woodrats, Will called me "rat man." When I was working on flying squirrels, he called me "squirrel man." He was in his early forties at this time, and he thoroughly considered every word spoken to him before replying. He lived in the caretaker's house in Camp Robinson, where he was born. He became caretaker of Robinson Forest in 1986 when Junior, caretaker since 1956, retired.

Junior was in his eighties. He was wearing his usual bib overalls. His face was tanned and deeply creased by a life exposed to weather. He spoke softly and slowly, yet had a quick wit and a dry sense of humor. Will told me that his father landed on Omaha Beach during the invasion of Normandy in 1944, but Junior did not talk about D-day. Junior had roamed these woods since 1935, and his memory of past fires was encyclopedic.

For several hours the history unfolded. First was the fire of 1936. Junior described how strong westerly winds blew a shower of embers from a distant fire into the forest. The embers ignited the three highest peaks south of Buckhorn Creek. The peak with Mart Rock ignited, then the peak with Miller Rock and a third peak straddling the southern boundary. The fires did not burn below fourteen hundred feet. As Junior described the details, Will pointed to the specific locations on the map and I made three circles in red ink along the fourteen-hundred-foot topographic lines and labeled them "fire of '36." Junior then continued with the fires of '52, '58, '60, and '81. Will pointed to locations on the map and I marked the path of each fire with a different color: black, green, blue, and yellow.

In pencil I labeled each fire and made notes. As the dates became more recent, Will interjected information as well. When we got to the most recent fires, Will provided most of the details while Junior listened and nodded in agreement.

One story stands out: the exploding maples of 1994. That year a fire burned east from Lewis Fork, up the slope, over the ridge, and down to Roaring Fork. The ridge had a thick stand of young red maples. Junior told me the fire was particularly hot and reminded me that young red maples have very thin bark. He explained that the extreme heat and lack of bark insulation brought the moisture inside the maples to a quick boil, and they exploded moments before the advancing fire reached them. Junior described trees exploding instantaneously from top to bottom, sending showers of sparks up and out in all directions. He said it was the only time he ever saw that happen. As with all of Junior's fire stories, I recorded the details in my field notebook.

Junior provided details of the path and direction of the flames for each fire he described. The fire of 1952, the largest in the forest's history, is a good example of the precision of his recall. It was an especially dry year. The fire resulted from a feud between a forest employee and a disgruntled inhabitant of a nearby hollow, although Junior did not know the basis of the feud. Apparently the local man abducted the employee's cat, tied a gasoline-soaked rag to its tail, lit the rag, and released the flaming cat into the dry forest, igniting a fire that quickly spread across the north and then down to Panther Creek. It did not cross the creek but moved southeast along the bank to Coles Fork. Then it traveled east for two miles before it jumped Coles Fork and went south into Flat Hollow. From there it continued south up and over the ridge, finally stopping at Bee Creek. By the time the fire was out, the northern half of Robinson Forest—six thousand acres—had burned.

As the afternoon progressed, the map filled with the colors of more recent fires. From time to time, Junior would wander as he reminisced about events not associated with fires. Will would allow this briefly before gently redirecting his father back to the fire we were discussing. I would resume marking paths of fires as the history continued: the fires of '93, '94, '95, '96, '99, and the "area of annual fire." The latter label indicated that fires are set so frequently in this area that marking the path of each was not possible. I marked these recent fires with brown, pink, purple, light blue, and gray markers. I eventually ran out of colors, so the fire of '99 was black crosshatching. As we continued, it became disturbingly clear that arson has been growing increasingly more common in Robinson Forest. We did not know, of course, that the fire of 2001 was only a few months away.

To satisfy my skepticism about Junior's ability to recall such precise details, a few days later I hiked five miles to Panther Creek, stopping at Flat Hollow and Bee Creek along the way to look for evidence supporting Junior's recollections. The trees to the south of Bee Creek were large and had the look of a forest approaching old growth. A misconception exists that "old growth" means uniform stands of extremely large trees; in fact, old-growth forests are complex in composition with a mix of trees ranging from small to extremely large. An old-growth forest includes gaps of open canopy where some of the giants that could no longer hold their footing in the thin topsoil toppled over during windstorms. Other giants that have long since fallen are slowly decomposing on the forest floor. This look of an old-growth forest was slowly coming to the area south of Bee Creek as well as some other areas of Robinson Forest, indicating that it was a maturing second-growth forest. North of Bee Creek, an area exposed to past fires according to Junior's recollections, trees were generally smaller, and the bases of the largest trees still showed burn scars. I found pieces of charcoal from some of the more recent fires. I visited several areas that Junior described as being at the edges of past fires, and every time, I found evidence confirming Junior's descriptions.

The most frequently burned area—the area Will had me mark as the area of annual fire—is along Lewis Fork Road near the western boundary of the forest. A public access road runs through this section of Robinson Forest, starting at the confluence of Lewis Fork and Buckhorn Creek and following the stream up the hollow past a cluster of houses officially designated as Noble, Kentucky. The road then veers east, away from the stream, up the slope, and out of the hollow onto a reclaimed surface mine. Locals have a habit of setting fires along this road. A large fire along Lewis Fork Road consumed seventy-five acres in early November

2001. I first saw the site two weeks later, and it was clear this had been an extremely hot fire. All of the mid-sized trees, the saplings, and the shrubs as well as fallen trees, branches, and leaf litter had been vaporized into a deep, loose layer of ash that turned my boots and jeans black as I waded through. The understory was denuded, and only the largest trees remained. Dead tree stumps and their roots had burned below the soil surface, leaving deep pits with horizontal chambers.

Six weeks after the fire, rain packed down the fluffy ash and washed the residue off stones and trash that had not seen sunlight for years, exposing the metal bases of shotgun shells and rusted cans. I found a four-foot piece of a broken cross saw, the tool loggers used to cut down trees before chain saws existed. This piece of history dated back one hundred years to the time when the Mowbray and Robinson Company was logging the forest.

Hickory nuts and acorns littered the ground, an indication that the trees did not release their mast until after the fire. The nuts and acorns stood out in sharp contrast to the black ash. For some big trees weakened by this and past fires, this was to be their last mast. Most, however, would survive, and even thrive, for many more years.

The abundance of easily visible food set off a feeding frenzy in the forest. White-tailed deer and turkeys were scrambling to eat as much as they could. Deer tracks and droppings and turkey scrapes were everywhere. Fresh excavations at the bases of large rocks littered with the debris of chewed acorns suggested that chipmunks survived the fire and were participating in the feeding frenzy as well. Before long, not a hickory nut or acorn remained. They had all been eaten or cached away.

Intermixed with the acorns were the shells of two species of native land snails: the spike-lipped crater, a snail the size of a silver dollar, and the dime-sized flat bladetooth. Strangely, none of the shells was burned, yet the snails within were dead. They survived the fire but died while crawling over the ash.

I looked for evidence of a small mammal called the hairy-tailed mole, using my boot to gently scrape the ash away to expose bare earth. With little effort this exposed meandering trails of elevated soil an inch and a half wide and less than an inch high, indicating that the tunnel was recently excavated just below the surface. I poked my index finger through the raised soil in several places to confirm a tunnel. The hairy-tailed mole, like the other five species of North American moles, is an evolutionary marvel adapted for life in dark, tight tunnels. Moles are fossorial; that is, they spend most of their lives underground. Their eyes are of little use there in the darkness and have become tiny organs hidden beneath fur. Moreover, natural selection has shaped the moles to "swim" through soil. Their bodies are streamlined to reduce friction. The soft, flexible fur can lie toward the head or toward the tail depending on whether the mole is moving backward or forward. The ears are mere openings buried beneath the fur, evolved to reduce drag and prevent soil from entering and damaging the middle ear. Wide front feet and powerful forearm and shoulder muscles permit rapid tunneling through soil.

The hairy-tailed mole plays a vital role in the survival of small animals escaping fire. With their adaptations for digging, hairy-tailed moles can rapidly create a vast tunnel network with tunnels both close to the surface and deep in the soil. Most of these are feeding tunnels that the mole uses only once. Many creatures survive forest fires by taking refuge in mole tunnels, including insects, worms, snails, crayfish, salamanders, lizards, small snakes, and mammals such as voles and shrews. Having refugees in its tunnel system benefits the mole as well. Although small, hairy-tailed moles are voracious carnivores capable of killing prey larger than themselves. An encounter with a mole is likely to be fatal for any creature small enough to take refuge in the tunnel system. Thus the dilemma the smallest of the forest creatures must face: the high probability of death by fire by not escaping into a tunnel versus the unknown, but lesser, probability of encountering a hungry mole. Escaping into the tunnel system is the better bet.

I have captured only one living hairy-tailed mole in all the years I have worked in Robinson Forest. I plucked it from the ground as it was repairing its tunnel, which I had intentionally collapsed. When I saw the soil being pushed up, I quickly plunged a shovel into the ground behind the mole and popped it out and into a wooden box. The pugnacious little predator snarled and hissed and shrieked at me, showing no fear. When I poked my finger (encased in a thick leather glove) into the box, the mole lunged, biting the glove and violently shaking its head while growling and refusing to release my finger. I pulled my hand out of the glove, which the mole continued to attack for five more minutes before succumbing to exhaustion.

A misconception exists that a forest is lifeless after fire. There was death, certainly, in the November 2001 fire. There was survival as well. Many root systems and seeds survived. Birds and large mammals simply flew or ran away to return later. Flying squirrels and gray squirrels took refuge in hollow cavities in the tallest trees far above the flames. Chipmunks hid in rock crevices and burrows. Salamanders, snails, snakes, lizards, pine voles, shrews, and white-footed mice took refuge in the tunnels of hairy-tailed moles, and also survived.

In addition, the fire released nutrients such as nitrogen back into the soil, stimulating new plant growth. In fact, many plants thrive following fire. Fire opens the canopy, permitting more sunlight to reach the ground, stimulating new growth. By the following April, spring flowers were thriving and seeds were germinating. Tender stems and leaves began to sprout up from surviving root systems. By midsummer the burned area was a vibrant green. Walking was easy for the first few months because the fire had removed obstacles such as fallen tree trunks and greenbrier tangles. By the summer of 2003, almost two years after the fire, saplings filled the open voids. Sassafras, sourwood, black gum, red maple, scarlet oak, and chestnut oak formed dense stands six to eight feet tall. Greenbrier and blackberry vines were denser than before the fire, their sharp thorns easily penetrating clothing and leaving legs and arms bloodied, scratched, and raw. In just two years the burned site transformed into a dense, lush, green jungle, demonstrating Robinson Forest's capacity to recover from fire.

Even though human-caused events such as fire can be beneficial, most of what we bring to forests is not. For example, the impact of humans on the American chestnut has been tragic. The American chestnut was once a dominant tree in eastern deciduous forests, including those on the Cumberland Plateau. Estimates suggest that 25 percent of all trees growing on the Appalachian Mountains were chestnuts. The American chestnut was a big, fast-growing tree; some trees growing in the best conditions reached heights of 150 feet with trunks up to 10 feet in diameter. These trees produced copious nuts that showered forest floors in the fall and were a significant food source for wildlife. White-tailed deer, wild turkeys, black bears, ruffed grouse, squirrels, mice, and many other rodents ate them. Allegheny woodrats and flying squirrels likely cached them in great numbers for winter food. The now extinct passenger pigeon, once the most abundant bird in the world, may have relied on chestnuts.

In the summer of 1904, American chestnut trees in what is now the Bronx Zoo in New York City began dropping their leaves while the surrounding trees remained green and lush. Orange-red spots appeared on the bark of American chestnuts but no other species. Branches began to die; then the trees themselves began to die. Dying chestnuts began to appear throughout the Bronx, then in Brooklyn. Two years would pass before William Murrill, staff mycologist at the New York Botanical Garden, identified the killer. What became known as the chestnut blight was caused by an Asian bark fungus (*Cryphonectria parasitica*) that hitched a ride on Asiatic chestnut trees imported into the United States. The fungus could enter the bark of a tree through any crack or hole. Once in, it spread under the bark, destroying the cambium and essentially girdling the tree. The orange-red spots on the bark were the fungi's reproductive structures, which released countless millions of spores into the air that infected other chestnuts. By 1908 the blight had spread to Pennsylvania, New Jersey, Virginia, and Maryland and was a full-blown epidemic spreading south through the Appalachian forests and the states to the east.

The blight was in eastern Kentucky by the late 1920s. I am not certain how tall Robinson's chestnuts were when the blight arrived. The stump sprouts were rebounding from Mowbray and Robinson's logging; thus the first chestnuts cut in 1912 had at least fifteen years of stump growth. These fast-growing trees were certainly putting on a lot of new wood each year. What I do know, because Junior Marshall told me (he witnessed the die-off), is that the last of Robinson's chestnuts were dead by 1939, as were billions of other American chestnuts in the eastern deciduous forests. Before the logging of Robinson began, American chestnuts were the most common trees on the upper slopes and may have accounted for 70 to 80 percent of the trees. Young chestnuts still sprout from those eighty-year-old parent stumps and grow quickly. Sadly, the blight infects and kills the young trees as they approach twenty feet. Time is quickly running out for the old root systems hidden beneath rotting chestnut stumps. Before long, new sprouts will cease to emerge from the forest floor.

We do not know how much more abundant wildlife was in eastern deciduous forests when American chestnuts thrived. We do know that clouds of passenger pigeons once covered the slopes of Robinson Forest. Massive flocks with millions of these big blue-and-red birds searched the forest floor for chestnuts and acorns. Foraging birds were leap-frogged by others that finished scouring the forest floor behind them, creating a blue-and-red cloud of pigeons rolling over the forest floor. Even if we had been conservation-minded in the late nineteenth century and had spared the passenger pigeon from extinction, the chestnut blight might have destroyed this bird all the same. We will never know.

With the chestnuts gone, other trees, including oaks and hickories, filled the void. Scattered among these trees lie massive blocks of sandstone. Like me, they are on a journey down the slope. Their trip will take millennia, though, while mine will take less than an hour. Some of these floating boulders have traveled all the way down from the ridgetops; others have joined more recently as they broke free from exposed sandstone seams. Obstacles slow a block's journey. Trees obstruct the path, bringing the block to a temporary halt. If a tree is young, yet large enough to resist being flattened, then the block must wait decades or centuries while the tree grows, matures, dies, and rots away, once again clearing the path. And during all those decades, freezing and thawing, wind and rain, expansion and contraction wear the block down. Lichens and mosses continue to gnaw away at it, turning rock into sand, and roots continue to pry the block apart.

On the lower slopes, another transition has taken place. The slopes are now wetter and cooler, the canopy is denser, and the understory is more shaded. American beeches abound here; the smooth, gray trunks of the largest ones look like the legs of giant elephants. The smaller beech trees in the understory hold their shriveled leaves through the winter until late spring. On gray winter days they look like small yellow-brown clouds drifting up the slopes. The lower slopes support a mosaic of forest communities, including the hemlock–mixed hardwood cove communities and the hemlock–beech–yellow-poplar ravine communities. The cove communities grow on wet benches above streams as well as in the large depressions that pox the lower slopes. In addition to beech, hemlock, and yellow poplar, these diverse communities feature sugar maple, yellow buckeye, basswood, various oaks, bitternut hickory, magnolias, walnut, pawpaw, and dogwood. Woodland ferns and spring flowers are especially abundant. Clonal stands of pawpaws can become quite dense in coves. These small understory trees produce the largest edible fruit of any native North American tree. The fruit has a rich yellow pulp filled with antioxidants and more protein than any other native fruit. Some say it tastes like a combination of custard and banana; others say mango and banana. Pawpaw fruits dangle from the tree's spindly branches until August and September, then drop to the forest floor, delighting the raccoons, foxes, squirrels, and other rodents that covet their energy- and nutrient-rich flesh. Finding a ripe pawpaw on a September hike through Robinson Forest is always a treat.

The densely shaded ravine communities are on the steepest lower slopes. Hemlocks and beeches dominate the acidic soils of this low-diversity community, especially the hemlocks, whose small, dark evergreen leaves and dense branches create the deep shade that defines ravines. Even on the hottest summer day the world beneath a hemlock is cool and comfortable. In the recorded history of Robinson Forest, dramatic loss of trees has so far been confined to the higher slopes, where pests destroyed pines and American chestnuts. The next likely threat could strike at any time and will target the hemlocks on the lower slopes. The hemlock woolly adelgid, an insect from Asia, sucks the sap from leaves and twigs of both the eastern hemlock and the Carolina hemlock. It has killed up to 90 percent of the hemlocks in Virginia, New Jersey, and Connecticut and has decimated the hemlocks of the southern Appalachians. Woolly adelgids arrived in Kentucky in 2006. I have been told that the pest was first found in Robinson in 2010. That discovery could be a death sentence. The dense stands of hemlocks that dominate ravines and cover the low, cool north-facing slopes are symbolic of Robinson Forest. Some are more than one hundred years old, survivors of Mowbray and Robinson's loggers and the many fires that have swept through the forest since. They are unlikely to survive the woolly adelgids.

Salamanders and small snakes favor the cool, wet lower slopes. Slimy salamanders, Cumberland Plateau salamanders, four-toed salamanders, and ravine salamanders prowl beneath the decaying leaves in search of small invertebrates. These small, slender amphibians absorb oxygen through skin kept moist by leaf litter and humus. They do not use their vestigial lungs to breathe. Snakes not much larger than earthworms also live beneath the leaf litter, although they are rarely seen. Northern red-belly snakes, worm snakes, smooth earth snakes, and ringneck snakes hunt beneath the leaves for small insects, earthworms, slugs, centipedes, and millipedes.

Among the rarest and most unusual amphibians in Robinson Forest is the four-toed salamander. This slender, three-inch-long salamander has a dark orange-brown back and a shiny, porcelain white belly with striking black blotches. The base of the tail is constricted, as if a string was tied around the tail and pulled too tight. As the name implies, each foot has four toes, which is unusual for salamanders. This beautiful little amphibian is unique in exhibiting parental care: females guard their eggs until their offspring hatch. Four-toed salamanders are not common, in large part because their breeding pools must possess a specific combination of conditions that is rare. Fallen, moss-covered logs or rocks must be in or near the edge of a pool, and the moss must sit loosely atop a layer of organic debris. Salamanders, unlike frogs and toads, have internal fertilization. Once the eggs are ripe, a female will crawl under the mat of moss and form a tiny den in the organic layer. Here she lays her eggs and then curls her body around them. The eggs are unusually large considering the small size of the mother. The yolk is white surrounded by a clear gelatinous outer layer. The larvae grow slowly. The mother remains vigilant, cleaning and protecting her eggs until they hatch. It is essential that the eggs be suspended above water. As they hatch, the larvae wriggle out from under the moss and drop into the water. The mother then departs, returning to her enigmatic life on the forest floor. Where four-toed salamanders go and what they do when not breeding is a mystery. In twenty years, I have found only one in the leaf litter away from a breeding pool.

Centipedes and millipedes thrive in the moist leaf litter of the lower slopes. The largest in Robinson Forest is the North American millipede (*Narceus americanus*). This slow-moving, four-inch-long arthropod is a striking creature. The rings that make up its rounded body are black, purple, or red (sometimes orange or yellow). Its many legs are burgundy red. Millipedes are easy to find as they crawl over the moist forest floor. When disturbed, they curl up into a flat coil, looking like a brightly colored cinnamon roll, and release a benzoquinone compound that is believed to repel predators. My first trip to Robinson Forest in 1991 was also my first encounter with this millipede. I picked it up for a better look. To my surprise, the coiled millipede gave off a pleasing odor—like maraschino cherries. Since then, I pick up every *Narceus* I find and gently shake it until the millipede emits the aroma. *Narceus* is responsible for one of my most embarrassing moments.

Wayne Davis is a classic old-school naturalist who came to the University of Kentucky in the 1950s. He is the author of a number of books, including *Bats of North America*, a classic well known by all who study mammals. Wayne spent a lot of time in Robinson Forest in the 1960s, and I had the honor and pleasure of his company on several of my early trips to the forest. Wayne is slight in stature, soft-spoken, and vastly knowledgeable about Robinson's ecology, and he taught me a lot about the natural history of the forest. One day, Wayne noticed my habit of shaking and sniffing every *Narceus* I found. He looked at me with a serious expression and quietly said that one of the best-kept secrets in the world was that the flavoring of maraschino cherries comes from this millipede. It had to remain a secret, he said, because consumption of these cherries would plummet if word got out and the industry would be destroyed. I looked at Wayne in disbelief; he nodded, his expression dead serious. I sniffed several more millipedes that day; each smelled exactly like maraschino cherries. I felt proud that Wayne had shared the secret with me. Years later, I was doing research in an area of western Kentucky called Land between the Lakes, and Bill Snyder, a biologist from Austin Peay State University, was showing me around. We came upon a *Narceus*; he picked it up, shook it, and sniffed. I was amazed to discover that I was not the only person who did this. To impress him with my deep grasp of natural history, I shared the great secret Wayne had told me. Bill dropped the millipede, stiffened his spine, glowered at me, and said, "Maraschino cherries are flavored with amandine, you fool!" Then he turned and walked away. Only then did I realize that Wayne Davis was a prankster and I was painfully gullible. Wayne set a trap many years earlier that I stepped into in western Kentucky. I felt its cold, hard jaws snap shut as I was called a fool. I have shared Wayne's "secret" with my own students. I'm not sure how many still eat maraschino cherries.

Possibly the most common mammal of Robinson Forest is also one of the most secretive, rarely seen even by those who spend a lot of time in the forest. It is found up and down the slopes but prefers the lower slopes where the cover is densest. Every night, southern flying squirrels emerge to search for nuts and acorns. Unlike Robinson's other squirrels (woodchucks, chipmunks, and gray squirrels), which forage by day, flying squirrels are active by night, gliding from tree to tree to avoid foxes, coyotes, raccoons, copperheads, timber rattlesnakes, and other predators on the forest floor. By being active at night, they avoid avian predators that hunt by day. Of the 280 species of squirrels that exist worldwide, 40, including Robinson's flying squirrel, are nocturnal gliders. Most of these species live in Southeast Asia; many are threatened or endangered by deforestation. Two species occur in Eurasia; of these, the Siberian flying squirrel is endangered. Of the two species that live in North America, the northern flying squirrel is considered endangered in the southern Appalachians. By contrast, the southern flying squirrel is thriving.

Flying squirrels look nothing like their relatives the gray squirrels. They are much smaller, for one thing. Loose flaps of skin on each side of the body called gliding membranes, or more properly "patagia," connect the wrist and ankle. The flying squirrel controls these membranes with a spur of cartilage attached to each wrist and connected to small muscles. When leaping from a tree, the flying squirrel fully extends the front legs forward and the hind legs backward. By flipping the spurs out away from its body, it tightens and expands the patagia to catch more air and extend the glide. The squirrel flexes the spurs according to how far and how fast it wishes to glide. A flying squirrel has a small, light body that flattens while it is gliding and a wide, flat tail that is used as a rudder. The face is rounded, with big black eyes that seem out of proportion with the small head. Of the hundreds of students who have live-trapped mammals with me at Robinson, not one has found flying squirrels anything less than adorable. I have trapped more than three hundred flying squirrels during my time in Robinson Forest, and I still feel the same way.

Very few people are lucky enough to see a flying squirrel glide out from the canopy in the morning light. The three hundredth glide was as mesmerizing to me as the first. Some glide hundreds of feet down the slopes on their flights, some a few dozen feet to the nearest tree. Even the shortest glide is breathtaking.

I have a routine for releasing flying squirrels that generally results in a good glide. After all my students have had a chance to hold the trap and see the beautiful little creature up close, we look for a very tall, thin tree free of snags and hollow cavities where the squirrel might hide. I hold the trap against the tree with the door facing up, and then I open the door. The squirrel is out and onto the tree in a flash. It runs upward twenty feet or so, then flattens its body against the trunk. Flying squirrels are surprisingly well camouflaged when motionless. A flying squirrel out in the open in daylight must examine its surroundings and assess its next move while avoiding a predator's attention. After a few motionless minutes, the little squirrel will race up the tree toward the canopy, then quickly flip its body so its head is facing down. No longer flattened, the flying squirrel is alert now and looking around, perhaps for familiar trees, especially big trees with cavities and snags. The squirrel usually surveys the forest for several minutes. If not satisfied, it will run farther up the tree for a better view.

Often it runs toward the top of a tree, stopping just below the canopy. Again flipping the body so the head is facing down, the squirrel slowly looks left and right, then locks onto its intended target and freezes in place. My students and I hold our breath waiting for the squirrel to make its next move. Then it happens. The squirrel launches, sailing out into the air over our heads. Body flat, legs fully extended, patagia stretched tight, wrist spurs flexed out, flat tail gently tilting right and left. Every student gasps. Expletives fill the forest air: "Wow!" "Amazing!" "Holy shit!" and

"Holy crap!" Every glide is unique and amazing. It is a spectacular thing to see anytime, but especially on a winter morning when the leaves are down and the morning sun gives the forest a golden yellow glow. As the squirrel glides over our heads, the bright blue sky accentuates its rectangular outline. Its feet and toes are clearly visible. Its little head moves from side to side in flight as it studies the forest rushing past.

As the squirrel approaches its target tree, the back legs and tail drop as the body shifts out of its horizontal plane to a vertical position parallel with the approaching tree. The landing is soft. The flying squirrel freezes for a moment, then dashes up the tree. If the tree has a cavity, the squirrel vanishes inside it. More often, the first target tree is not the final destination but a staging point from which the squirrel launches again toward the final tree, likely its home, where its nest and cache of nuts and acorns are located. After the first launch, I tell my students to keep their eyes on the squirrel because the second launch is even more spectacular. The squirrel usually lands on a tree taller than the original tree where we released it, providing an even higher point for the launch. The second launch comes quickly. Before my students have time to recover from the first glide, the squirrel is in the air again. Another volley of expletives erupts. This glide is longer and ends with the squirrel disappearing into a hole immediately upon landing.

Flying squirrels have precise control of their speed and direction. This is amazing considering that flying squirrels do not fly, and in fact technically do not even glide. They are performing a controlled fall. And in control they are! I have watched squirrels cut sharp 90-degree turns right or left as they recalculate their target tree in midflight. One of the most spectacular glides I ever saw was by a flying squirrel released near the top of a slope. It launched and headed full-speed downhill, parallel with the slope. After sailing 150 feet down the slope, the squirrel made an abrupt 180-degree turn, landed on the snag of a huge white oak it had already passed, and vanished into a cavity. Either the squirrel overshot its original target or it caught sight of a suitable cavity midflight. Either way, it was a striking example of the control these nimble little mammals have.

Living in the canopy and gliding from tree to tree at night has its advantages. Flying squirrels escape the hawks that hunt by day, the snakes that silently pursue other rodents on the forest floor, and predatory mammals unable to climb trees. I have set many thousands of live traps on the forest floor over the years, but I have never caught a flying squirrel in one. It's a different story if I nail an open jar of peanut butter to a tree a foot above the ground. Photos from wildlife cameras aimed at the jar have captured as many as five flying squirrels around the jar at one time feasting on peanut butter yet avoiding contact with the ground. Sequences of photos show that the squirrels retreat up the tree trunk when skunks, raccoons, or gray foxes arrive at the jar, and return only after the predators depart.

Yet flying squirrels cannot avoid all predators by staying in the trees. Rat snakes are expert climbers and can find cavities fifty feet and more up a tree. The higher a squirrel's nest is above the ground, the better are the odds its helpless young will not become a meal for a snake. The biggest threat to adult flying squirrels in Robinson Forest is the barred owl, a large nocturnal hunter that flies under the canopy and between the trees. A barred owl can pluck a flying squirrel off a tree trunk before the squirrel knows it is coming. Flying squirrels prefer areas where trees are closer together and where the canopy is dense and closed. The advantage is clear. The denser the trees, the more difficult it is for barred owls to maneuver and attack, and the greater the likelihood that a cavity is available nearby. Shorter glides from tree to tree reduce the chances of being picked off by an owl in midglide. The harder it is for an owl to maneuver, the easier it is for a flying squirrel to escape.

One of the sounds that most defines Robinson Forest is the haunting call of a barred owl at dusk: "Who cooks for you . . . who cooks for you . . . who cooks for you all." When I hear a barred owl call, I feel a warm sense of being immersed in nature. The call tells me I am in my serene forest far from the crush of urban living. But it must be a terrifying sound to a flying squirrel, because the call of the barred owl announces that the predator is near and the risk of death is great.

By the time I arrive at the base of the slope, my journey has taken me past most of Robinson's 60 species of trees, some common and others rare. During my descent I may have passed 8 species of oak, 5 species of hickory, 4 maples, 3 pines, 3 magnolias, 2 ashes, 2 elms, and 2 walnuts as well as black gum, sweet gum, sourwood, pawpaw, and sassafras. I probably also passed American hornbeam, hop-hornbeam, flowering dogwood, Allegheny serviceberry, redbud, and American holly along the way. At the base of the slope I find that many floating blocks of sandstone have ended their journey down the slope here as well. My journey lasted an hour; theirs took tens of thousands to tens of millions of years. I am sweaty and dirty, scratched and scraped, but still in one piece. The blocks, on the other hand, are no longer massive pieces of sandstone. The agents of erosion and the passage of time have reduced them to a rubble field of rocks, gravel, and sand. For these pieces of sandstone now scattered along the edge of a stream at the base of a slope, one journey has ended and the next is about to begin. These journeys are all part of the larger rock cycle that never ends.

CHAPTER 5

Thinking Like a Forest

Erik Reece

If you stand at the top of the fire tower in Robinson Forest and look around, as I have often done, your gaze will slowly register a strange and most unnatural contrast—the most biologically diverse forest in North America is surrounded by nearly barren plateaus created by mountain-top-removal strip mining (MTR). From the fire tower you can see that Robinson Forest is an island of life surrounded by a ring of death: the laws of nature hemmed in by the unnatural hubris of the industrial mind.

Because the strip mine is a product of the industrial mind, it embodies many of our planet's most urgent problems. Strip mining—the most expedient, and most environmentally damaging, way to mine coal—quickens climate change faster than any other human activity; it buries headwater streams and leaches toxic heavy metals into downstream drinking water supplies; the denuded mountainsides it creates accelerate erosion and flooding; and the forest fragmentation that results has sent two-thirds of the Cumberland Plateau's 250 species of songbirds into decline. But MTR continues (as of this writing) because it is the fastest and cheapest method of rooting coal from the ground. And because Americans consume three times as much coal today as we did in 1970, MTR has bled out across the Appalachian Mountains and the Cumberland Plateau, destroying more than five hundred ranges and 1.4 million acres. In Kentucky alone it has buried more than two thousand miles of streams and polluted twenty-five hundred more miles of streams. Environmental biologist Gregory Pond found that blasting and subsequent dumping of "overburden"—that is to say, any part of a mountain that is not coal—had impaired 95 percent of the streams surrounding surface mines in eastern Kentucky. A 2011 paper in the journal *Science* reported that MTR discharges dangerous levels of heavy metals such as magnesium and selenium into mountain streams. These pose a severe threat to aquatic life at the headwaters and to human life downstream, where family wells show traces of those toxic chemicals and drinking water is overloaded with heavy metals such as lead, arsenic, and beryllium.

What is more, the Appalachian Regional Commission reported that the counties that have seen the most strip mining remain the poorest counties in the entire Appalachian range, indeed in the United States. A recent Gallup study found that of all the 435 congressional House districts, Kentucky's 5th District, which surrounds Robinson Forest, is the sickest—both physically and psychologically—in the entire country. Physician Michael Hendryx's research has shown that as mining increases in Appalachian counties, poverty and unemployment rise. Men and women living in heavily mined areas are far more likely to die prematurely of heart, respiratory, and kidney disease than residents living beyond the coalfields. More shocking still, Hendryx found that birth defects in Appalachian communities near strip mines are *42 percent higher than in non-strip-mining communities.*

Like Nigeria, Chad, and Sudan, central Appalachia is a region as poor in tangible health and wealth as it is rich in natural resources. Harvard economists Jeffrey Sachs and Andrew Warner labeled this volatile combination "the resource curse." Powerful corporations move into a poor region, extract and export its resources, internalize the profits, and externalize the damage of extraction. The end result of the resource curse in Appalachia is too often characterized by another sociological phenomenon—the tragedy of the commons. The water, mountains, and air, which should be a shared inheritance, are polluted by corporations that take what isn't theirs and leave behind toxic waste that should not be ours. A front-page photograph in the *New York Times* in 2010 showed seven-year-old Ryan Massey, whose deteriorating teeth have almost all been capped.

Reporter Charles Duhigg discovered that the Massey family's drinking water contains high levels of barium, lead, and manganese. Since 2004, coal operators around the Masseys' home have injected 1.9 billion gallons of coal waste into abandoned underground mine shafts. Three of the larger operators even reported to state officials that 93 percent of the waste they injected into the ground contained illegal concentrations of the heavy metals that scoured the enamel off Ryan Massey's teeth and caused lesions to appear on the skin of his six-year-old brother. The reason the companies reported their own violations is because they knew the Environmental Protection Agency would not hold them accountable for their crimes, at least not in any serious way. The small fines the EPA imposes for such infractions are simply written off as the cost of doing dirty business.

In *What My Heart Wants to Tell*, Verna Mae Slone maintained that God set down his hardiest people in the Appalachian Mountains because he knew they would need strong and deep resolve to get their living from this hard land. And indeed, one could argue that they formed a stronger attachment to the land than any other European settlers in North America. But over the past one hundred years, the industrialists have gone to extraordinary lengths to sever the connections between the people and the land. They have gradually sacrificed the mountains so the rest of the country can fill bigger houses with bigger TVs. Children like Ryan Massey don't get much thought.

One symbol of that severance is a small family cemetery that stands in stark isolation right in the middle of the sprawling strip mine north of Robinson Forest. It is called the Flint Hill Cemetery, and because federal law mandates that coal operators cannot strip-mine within one hundred feet of a burial ground, that single green knoll, surrounded by thousands of acres of flattened ridgelines, is the only remaining evidence of a mountain spur called Flint Ridge. The ridge has been leveled all the way from the cemetery to the boundary of Robinson Forest.

One Sunday afternoon, I drive along Buckhorn Creek and up to the Flint Hill Cemetery. The paved road that leads through a small valley community gives way to a gravel haul road, cut wide to accommodate coal trucks. I follow it up to the mine site's empty guard shack. There I take a hard left, bumping along through black puddles before I find the narrow road that leads up to the cemetery. A few pines and poplars grow along the flanks of this knob, the only signs of life left in what was once a broadleaf forest. I stop and set my parking brake beside a white cinder-block chapel and walk up to where the dead crowd together, refugees at the top of this half-acre island. Many of them are descendants of the Millers, who settled Clemons Fork and Coles Fork in the 1800s. Some of the headstones date back to the Spanish-American War and the Civil War. Almost half of them appear homemade, molded out of cement. *N*s and *S*s are often written backward, and the spelling is in many cases phonetic. An unsettling but unsurprising number of the dead are children. Viola Grace's stone reads:

> BARnD MAY28
> 1910 DECESTED
> JULY 13 1911

Another is inscribed:

> LINVILL MCINToSh
> BORNAPRiL3 1910
> D.C. JUNE14 1920
> hE IS NOT dEd
> BUT ISLEEPINg

If ten-year-old Linvill McIntosh is indeed sleeping, it must be a restless slumber. He had to endure all of the blasting that brought down Flint Ridge. And now, about a hundred yards from his grave stand four fifty-foot-tall tipples where coal is unloaded, crushed, and processed along loud conveyer belts, then loaded back into huge coal trucks that rumble in and out of the mine site all day during the week. A slurry pond that sits to the left of the processing plant holds all of the chemical flocculants used to wash the coal before it is shipped to power plants across the country and abroad. Nineteen of those chemicals are cancer-causing agents; twenty-four are linked to lung and heart disease. This is a relatively small pond, but it is still filled with the same black sludge that in 2000 broke through an underground mine shaft in Martin County, Kentucky, and flooded valley communities. More than three hundred thousand gallons of the slurry poured down into Coldwater Creek and Wolf Creek, a spill thirty times larger than the *Exxon Valdez* disaster. It took the *New York Times* months to even mention the Martin County flood, leading one Wolf Creek resident to conclude, "I guess we're just not as cute as those otters."

Up at Linvill McIntosh's grave, I sense the same combination of neglect and disrespect for a region and its people. One weekday last year, when I came to the cemetery and listened to the noise of the trucks and the tipple, I remembered the Thomas Hardy poem "Channel Firing." In it, the deceased who lie buried in an English churchyard hear gunnery practice out at sea. Thinking it must be Judgment Day, they sit upright in their coffins, ready to be transfigured. But alas, the Almighty calls down to them that no, they are only hearing "nations striving strong to make / Red war yet redder." What is more, says the Lord,

That this is not the judgment-hour
For some of them's a blessed thing,
For if it were they'd have to scour
Hell's floor for so much threatening . . .

I don't know if coal operators are going to have to scour the floors of Hell for decimating the mountains of eastern Kentucky, though I have heard coalfield activists quote the passage from Revelation 11:18 that prophesies "the time for destroying the destroyers of the earth." When it comes to destroying the natural world, there are certainly few human impulses that rival the brutality and finality of mountaintop removal. Which makes this cemetery seem like an appropriate place to puzzle over the question of why the 85 percent of Americans who profess to be Christians so often fail or refuse to recognize some connection between a Creator and the creation. I wonder why so many Christians, especially in Kentucky, who identify themselves as "creationists" have made so little effort to protect the creation itself. I don't believe it is merely a question of semantics. As I write, one creationist organization called Answers in Genesis is developing plans for a theme park in northern Kentucky based on the biblical account of Noah's Ark. Creationists believe literally in the story of the Flood, and yet one lesson that can be drawn from that story is that Noah was the world's first conservationist. But I have never seen the argument to prove the existence of the Ark extended to the logical concern that right now, because of human pressures, the very species that Noah supposedly saved are going extinct—so says the World Resources Institute—at a rate of four per hour. And in North America, nothing destroys species habitat faster and more permanently than mountaintop removal.

Why do so many who believe in the divine creation of the world have so little to say in support of its preservation? Why is their love for the Creator so detached from their concern for the creation? Why are they not awestruck, as was Job, when the voice in the whirlwind detailed the astonishing diversity of this rare planet?

Perhaps the most common answer to those questions points all the way back to Genesis, which says that Yahweh gave the first humans "domin-ion" over the world. I have often heard coal operators cite the "dominion" passage as their rationale for tearing apart the mountains of Appalachia. But this strikes me as a flimsy justification for their real motive—love of money, which, according to the Apostle Paul, is the root of all evil. Of course, if we are honest with ourselves, we must admit that such avarice extends far beyond the coalfields and has created an American economy and an American popular culture that seem far less devoted to the Sermon on the Mount and far more grounded in the Seven Deadly Sins. The version of Christianity that we as a nation seem to prefer will forgive us those sins and rescue us up into the Sweet Hereafter, but it will not teach us, as Jesus urged in the Gospel of Luke, how to see *this world*, the natural world, as the Kingdom of God. We pump five billion pounds of toxic chemicals into the creation every year. And we use the coal from mountains like Flint Ridge to feed the power plants—the same ones William Blake called "the dark Satanic mills"—that are melting Arctic ice sheets and setting the world on fire.

We need a new story, a new creation story. Perhaps it should begin with this passage from a Wendell Berry poem:

There are no unsacred places.
There are only sacred places,
and desecrated places.

From where I am sitting in this cemetery I can see the desecration of Flint Ridge all around me, yet in the distance I also can see what Berry might call the sacred groves of Robinson Forest rising up against the horizon. And this view of the forest and the lines of Berry's poem lead me to an idea: since evolution has shown us that the entire chorus of life, millions upon millions of species, shares one common ancestor that lived 3.5 billion years ago, why not admit in our churches and schools and political theaters that human beings are *literally, genetically kin to all other living creatures*. In terms of both conservation and religion, this strikes me as one of the most hopeful and inspiring places to begin a new creation story—a place not of separation and exile but of interdependence and affection. That this idea also has demonstrable, empirical merit seems to me a beautiful confluence of the sciences and the humanities, perhaps even of agnostics and believers.

I walk down to my truck and start off across the strip mine toward Robinson Forest. The dry, hot air whips through my windows as I traverse this human-made savanna, comprised mainly of an exotic legume called lesbedeza and the exotic trees autumn olive and tree of heaven. No native hardwoods grow here except a few black locusts, and certainly no native orchids, herbs, or ferns could survive in this harsh ground depleted of topsoil and shade. What is here now wasn't here before, and what was here before won't ever come back. After about a mile, the boundaries of Robinson Forest come into view—made obvious by the vertical wall of sandstone that rises from the strip mine up to the trees. Indeed, this is the only forest I know of that a person might actually *fall off*.

The abrupt boundary does, however, dramatize one of the worst ecological effects of strip mining—and one of the most important reasons for preserving Robinson Forest. It is largely because of forest fragmentation that one can hear the cerulean warbler singing deep within Robinson Forest but almost nowhere else in eastern Kentucky. This particular songbird is so rare and wears such stunning blue plumage that Jonathan Franzen turned it into a fairly major character in his novel *Freedom*. In the background of that unhappy-family story lurks the complicated politics of mountaintop removal, and it is clear that Franzen did his homework, right down to the plight of the cerulean warbler. He knows this species is a forest obligate, which means it needs a large, undivided tract of woods as protection from predators and from the parasitism of female cowbirds, which lay their eggs in the nests of other birds. So, in varying degrees, do many of the other songbirds of the Cumberland Plateau, which explains why the populations of two-thirds of them are in decline throughout central Appalachia. In *Freedom*, the environmental lawyer Walter Berglund embarks on a rather misguided plan to re-create cerulean warbler habitat by reforesting strip mines. In a more realistic (though perhaps less dramatic) narrative, he would have had better luck saving the warbler by trying to save a place like Robinson Forest from being strip-mined in the first place.

Because Robinson Forest is the largest contiguous forest in Kentucky that still retains its preindustrial character, it is in many ways the last and best refuge for many native species threatened by forest fragmentation. Essentially, forest fragmentation is evolution in reverse: it chokes out species by reducing their habitat to small islands. In general, the larger an island—say, Madagascar—the larger the number of species that will evolve there. According to this theory of island biogeography, which was developed by E. O. Wilson and R. H. MacArthur back in 1967, the greater the area of a forest island, the greater the number of species within it. The smaller the island, the more inbreeding, the more predation from the edges, and the more parasitism by species like the cowbird. Because of Robinson Forest's long perimeter and deep cover—and because of its size and age—it represents one of Appalachia's best antidotes to the ravages of fragmentation, even while they surround the island-forest on all sides.

I lock my truck and climb the steep slope until I reach the completely vertical boundary of Robinson Forest. The groves of scrawny autumn olive abruptly give way to larger native oaks. Looking down to get my footing, I spot a borehole, about ten inches in diameter, drilled years ago deep into the sandstone so a core sample could be taken to determine where the coal seams lay and how deep they ran. I reach for the root of a chestnut oak and pull myself up onto the edge of the forest. The trunk of the tree has been marked with a blue-and-white blaze, UK's colors. Just beyond it lies a south-facing rock shelter—at least the part of it that hasn't been blasted apart. I duck underneath and look in its crevices for evidence of an Allegheny woodrat. Instead I find a phoebe's nest fastened to one rock wall. With her bill, the female phoebe threw mud against the vertical surface, to which she plastered moss. As a final touch, she lined her nest with a cushion of moss on which to lay and incubate four or five white eggs. It's an admirable piece of architecture and a reminder that what we call "wild" is really only a form of domesticity that we do not understand.

My footsteps rouse a raccoon that scurries up the back side of a large white oak. Six wild turkeys start sprinting down the hillside until a few of them rise into the air, crashing through the understory in their awkward flight. Farther into the forest a ruffed grouse is drumming its wings; behind me, from a distant mine site, I hear blasting.

Soon I reach the head of an ephemeral stream where the contour of this slope suddenly plunges like an overloaded bookshelf snapped in half. Much of central Appalachia is a landscape of dramatic folds, of falling rocks and falling water. Gravity is the highest law here, and it pulls me down into the streambed just as it pulls the stream. Only the swallowtail butterflies that flit back and forth over the water seem immune to gravity's pull. A long rock scarp forms a wall on one side, and stinging nettles and ferns cover the other steep bank. Hemlocks cling with exposed roots to the rock wall. Above them, on the underside of a rock shelter overhang, I can just barely make out the fossilized remains of a *Lepidodendron* tree. The black, striated lines are the impressions of fernlike leaves that locked away solar energy for hundreds of millions of years—until 1712, exactly three hundred years ago, when that energy was released by British inventor Thomas Newcomen, who figured out that he could power the first steam engine by burning the fossil trees—that is to say, by burning coal.

I step slowly over slick stones covered in emerald moss. In several places, fallen limbs have filtered leaves out of the current and turned them into thin humus where umbrella magnolia saplings have taken root. My own path down to Clemons Fork meanders as circuitously as the stream, which today runs low and quiet around the rocks and under the fallen trees. It's good company, this body of water, this eternal transient that, like the human self, is at once always and never quite the same. I gaze downstream where mature beech, hemlock, and poplar rise high from the banks until their canopies lean into one another like the long arch of a cathedral. I stop for a moment and stand still. The forest is absolutely quiet. It is a pregnant kind of silence, and I think, as I often do in Robinson Forest, of those ancient Chinese poets who once wandered mountains much like these. They were the world's first "nature writers," solitary men and women who found their poems in just such places— poems that praised the mountains and streams, poems that praised the silence out of which such poetry arose. While the flora and the landscape of central Appalachia resemble the mountains of southern China where Li Po and Tu Fu wrote their famous poems, that silence becomes harder and harder to find. The American poet Mary Oliver seemed to have felt that modern frustration when she wrote:

Wherever I am, the world comes after me.
It offers me its busyness. It does not believe
that I do not want it. Now I understand
why the old poets of China went so far and high
into the mountains, then crept into the pale mist.

The Chinese government built the massive Three Gorges Dam in the Wu Mountains that Li Po and Tu Fu once wandered, while here in the Appalachians, explosions destroy the silence, and the mountains, each day. In his book *Big Coal*, Jeff Goodell noted how Mao Tse-tung's injunction to "conquer nature" resulted in massive deforestation, erosion, and starvation across China, and alienated an entire generation from the natural world. A similar kind of estrangement has occurred in the mountains of Appalachia. You see it in the omnipresent FRIENDS OF COAL bumper stickers and you hear it in the thunderous applause at the statehouse when Kentucky governor Steve Beshear, in his "State of the Commonwealth" speech, demanded that the Environmental Protection Agency "get off our backs."

Unfortunately, Robinson Forest is not immune to the human urge to conquer nature. In fact, when I climb up the eastern flank of this hollow and look down into the next watershed, I see one of the most depressing signs of the conqueror—a clear-cut that stretches all the way down to a stream called Booker Fork.

In the summer of 2007, word leaked out around the University of Kentucky campus that the forestry department was planning to cut nearly a tenth of Robinson Forest to study the effects of logging on streams. The goal of this "streamside management zone" (SMZ) project was to develop best management practices (BMPs) that might provide guidelines—non-binding guidelines—for logging near streams throughout Kentucky. To prove that logging close to streams creates erosion and sedimentation, UK planned to do just that—cut eight hundred acres of steep riparian ridge sides in Robinson Forest. People were alarmed not only because the proposed method of logging amounted to a clear-cut (only a few trees per acre would be left), but because the logging would be done around one of the cleanest streams in Kentucky, Clemons Fork.

Supporters of the SMZ plan claimed that UK needed the money from the timber sale to continue funding the forest and the Robinson Scholars program. They also pointed out that E. O. Robinson clear-cut most of the forest in the 1920s, and the ecosystem had grown back as biologically diverse as it had originally been. But eighty years ago the forest was not surrounded by strip mines full of exotic species, as it is now. To log eight hundred acres would be to open a wide path for those invasive species to infiltrate the forest.

In October 2007, a group of UK students, along with Wendell Berry, requested a meeting with College of Agriculture dean Scott Smith. Berry and the students asked why the SMZ study had to be done in Robinson Forest, why it couldn't be done on land that more closely resembled real logging operations. They questioned the secrecy of the SMZ planning and asked why the College of Agriculture was given total decision-making power over a forest held in trust by the University of Kentucky for all the citizens of the state. And they asked why the research done in Robinson Forest had to be so destructive to its watersheds, why it had to follow the "destroy a village to save it" mentality that characterized another large-scale deforestation experiment, the Vietnam War.[1]

1. What follows is in no way meant as an attack on the character or the reputations of the people who proposed and conducted this research. As far as I know, they are first-rate scientists and scholars, and they have always treated me with civility and even generosity. I take issue not with the science but with where the project took place and the tenuous argument for its necessity.

Dean Smith's response to these concerns took the form of a warning. "If you stop this logging now," he told the activists, "you will be right back here in three years trying to stop the forest from being strip-mined."

When someone suggested that this was blackmail, Smith replied, "It's not blackmail. It's just the truth."

Truth or not, no one considered Smith's words an idle threat. But it was a no-win, two-pronged threat. On the one hand lay Smith's claim that if logging wasn't allowed, strip mining would be. On the other hand lay the concern that if the eight hundred acres were logged, coal operators could easily argue that since logging had already compromised part of the forest, the coal should be harvested as well for maximum revenue. Obviously, neither option would satisfy the conservationists in the room.

After the meeting, on September 4, 2007, Wendell Berry wrote Smith an open letter in which he pressed the matter: "The possibility that the forest will be strip-mined has been plainly in sight for several years, but it is hard to know what to make of it in its new manifestation as an either-or tradeoff. This seems to be a threat, but it is an obscure threat. Does it originate with you, or from somewhere higher in the University administration, or from somewhere in state government?" Wherever the threat was coming from, it offered Berry and his cohorts no good option, and so their only recourse was to oppose both the logging and the strip mining in Robinson Forest. "We must assume that the proposed clear-cut is not an alternative to strip mining," Berry wrote Smith, "but instead is the first step in a business plan that will culminate in strip mining." What is more, wrote Berry, "I feel sure, and for good reason, that the pressure on the forest is not scientific but financial."

After Berry's open letter came out, Representative Ben Chandler wrote to both the *Louisville Courier-Journal* and the *Lexington Herald-Leader* expressing his own opposition to the SMZ project. One of UK's major donors, Tracy Farmer, said he thought the logging would bruise UK's reputation and hurt future fundraising efforts. But UK president Lee Todd seemed unmoved and refused even to meet with the concerned students. They conducted various acts of nonviolent civil disobedience to get his attention, including a sit-in at the president's office, but in the end, Todd told the UK Board of Trustees, "We have a responsibility to do research in the forest." No one was questioning that, of course; the students were only questioning the kind of research being proposed. But in the summer of 2008, despite the fact that the bottom had fallen out of the timber market, UK went ahead with its plan to clear-cut eight hundred acres of Robinson Forest. The university grossed a mere $133,000 on the deal. That number divided by eight hundred acres, and divided again by eighty years of growth, amounts to a $2-per-acre profit.

I contemplate that shameful figure as I pick my way down through the thick blackberry brambles and greenbrier that have grown up here in the three years since the clear-cut. Poplar and umbrella magnolia saplings are inching skyward around the stumpage where the crowns of the fallen trees are scattered. A solitary towhee flits in and out of the discarded limbs. Some are banked to hold back erosion, but they appear to be having little effect. The entire ridge side feels unstable, torn asunder. It looks as if every inch of topsoil has been disturbed and exposed to the elements. A logging road is already beginning to wash out toward the stream, which feeds into Clemons Fork and is certainly adding to its turbidity. And large dead trees have been pushed down the banks, not left standing, as they should have been, for the towhee and other small forest dwellers. The few trees that were spared, mostly white oaks, look badly wind damaged.

I finally take a seat on a stump about three feet in diameter. I look across the stream to the opposite, uncut ridge. It is still densely textured with pines and oaks, ferns and wildflowers. It looks so obdurate, so stable, compared with this slope, which has been carved apart by bulldozers, skidders, and chain saws. Sitting here on this stump, I suddenly remember something the French novelist Guy de Maupassant said: He liked to eat lunch in the Eiffel Tower because it was the only place in Paris where he didn't have to *look at* the Eiffel Tower. I know what he means. Across the stream, graceful hemlocks and beeches cling to the lower slope and hold the topsoil in place. But this tree stump and everything around it represents the ugliness of the human industrial mind, and I find myself trying to look away.

Back in 2007, when the debate over the hillside was raging, various progressive voices brought up the Pioneer Forest in southern Missouri. The management practices at Pioneer were, they said, the opposite of the clear-cutting that would soon commence in Robinson Forest. Why, they asked, couldn't UK conduct research that resembled the work taking place in Missouri? Some in the UK forestry department dismissed the idea, arguing that what worked at Pioneer wouldn't work in Robinson because southern Missouri is flat and eastern Kentucky is steep. But the more I heard about the Pioneer Forest, the more I wanted to see it for myself.

So one day in the summer of 2011, Jim Krupa and I drove west through the recently flooded cornfields of Indiana and Illinois, got lost in St. Louis, then finally found our way south to Salem, Missouri. Early the next morning we met up with Pioneer's forest manager, Terry Cunningham. A tall, gregarious man, Cunningham has been on staff at Pioneer for thirty-nine years, and in 2009 he was named Missouri's Conservationist of the Year. Jim and I climbed into his truck, and the three of us headed out to explore the largest privately owned forest in Missouri. In the decades after Prohibition, these 154,000 acres were devoted, like Robinson Forest, largely to whiskey. National Distillers harvested much of the white oak for barrel staves. In 1954 St. Louis businessman Leo Drey bought the land and renamed it the Pioneer Forest (anyone who has purchased Drey canning jars probably made some small contribution to the acquisition). At that time, the national forests' management policy was shifting toward clear-cuts, but Drey resisted the trend and devoted Pioneer to what has come to be called "uneven-aged forest management" or "single-tree selection."

Sixty-five years later, the results of that policy were on display as we drove along the forest roads with Cunningham. There were no pine plantations like the ones we had seen driving in on Route 68—woodlots that Cunningham told us can support only 5–10 percent of the wildlife native to this area. The woods we were passing consisted of three distinct age classes of trees, made up predominantly of white oaks, red oaks, and shortleaf pines, respectively. That is to say, though Pioneer has been managed—and managed for profit—for more than six decades, it still retains the native composition and diversity of a southern Missouri forest.

Foresters enter a particular tract of land here every fifteen to twenty years and mark fewer than 40 percent of its trees to be removed. The general guiding principle is that the worst trees get cut and the healthiest trees remain. "If a tree would last for another ten years (or until the next scheduled harvest)," former Pioneer forester Russ Noah once said, "don't cut it." If a tree shows signs of infestation, disease, or storm damage, it gets removed. A tree that has reached its maximum stage of growth (around eighty years for red oaks and two hundred years for white oaks) is a likely candidate for the sawmill. In any given year, no more than 3 percent of the entire forest is cut. As a result of these practices, the total volume of wood in the Pioneer Forest has *tripled* since Leo Drey purchased it. In 1952 there were 1,128 board feet per acre in the forest; in 2007 that volume had climbed to 3,985 board feet.

The main economic objective of the Pioneer Forest is to encourage and increase the growth of the forest's most important native trees and its most marketable trees, both of which happen to be the oaks and pines. Under even-age management—that is to say, clear-cutting—growing oaks and pines is easy because both trees thrive in sunlight. And that is the chief objection to the management practices of the Pioneer Forest—oaks don't grow in the shade. The Pioneer foresters have balanced the economic value of growing oaks and pines with the ecological and aesthetic values of maintaining the woodland character of a sustainable forest. They do this by carefully examining the composition of each woodlot set for a harvest. Then they mark individual trees that are ready to be cut and whose removal will open part of the understory to sunlight. Because oaks have a tremendous taproot, they can wait years, even decades, for such an opening to occur.

Cunningham pulled off the dirt road beside a recently harvested tract, and we stepped out to see this policy in practice. He pointed to the stump where a scarlet oak had been cut, then to an oak sapling that had broken through the leaf litter about thirty yards away. "That smoldering oak pops as soon as light enters the forest," he explained. From the young oak's point of view, it was just waiting for a tree to fall or for fire to clear away part of the canopy. Thus, by cutting an old or sickly tree, the foresters and the loggers in the Pioneer are simply imitating the forest's natural processes.

I asked Cunningham if the Pioneer Forest philosophy could be compared to Wes Jackson's experiments at the Land Institute in Kansas, where mixed perennial grains are grown in a manner that emulates the natural diversity of the Great Plains, and in the process halts erosion, pesticide use, and the loss of biological diversity.

"Absolutely," he replied. "We're trying to mimic natural processes here." The Pioneer management policy simply represents an accelerated version of the changes that happen naturally within a forest. There is, after all, nothing natural about a clear-cut, but the death of individual trees is an elemental part of a forest's life cycle, reflected in Pioneer's method of single-tree selection. Such a philosophy requires as much art as it does science, Cunningham told us. The science lies in maintaining the forest's diversity and increasing its volume; the art takes place where art always begins—in the particulars. That is to say, individual foresters at Pioneer decide acre by acre which trees stay and which trees go. In a further attempt to mimic natural processes, foresters leave snag trees (standing dead trees) because they provide habitat for wildlife. As a result, E. M. Annand and F. R. Thompson found hooded warblers and northern parula warblers to be far more abundant in the Pioneer Forest than in surrounding forests that had been exposed to clear-cuts. Overall, the Pioneer retains far more habitat for native wildlife, and unlike tree plantations, its managers don't use herbicides to maintain an unnatural monoculture. Research has also shown that uneven-aged forests are less susceptible to tree mortality and less prone than clear-cuts to extensive, hot-burning forest fires. And because it preserves shade, selective harvesting keeps out invasive species of trees.

As for erosion, Cunningham drove us to a recent clear-cut in the Mark Twain National Forest where loggers had dragged their skidders indiscriminately across the woodlot, making no attempt to preserve the topsoil or limit damage. Then we stopped at a current harvest within the Pioneer where loggers practice "directional falling," ensuring that each felled tree causes as little damage as possible to the remaining stand. Then the loggers follow a skidding pattern that in some ways mimics the veins of a leaf: they drag each tree to a main artery, then pull it uphill, using marked trees as fulcrums for the skidding cables so as not to damage the trees that will remain. This method results in far less erosion than indiscriminate cutting and protects the soil from compaction and loss of nutrients. In addition, by opening only small sections of the forest canopy, uneven-age logging protects the topsoil's organic matter from the intense solar radiation that can kill fungi and bacteria and destabilize microscopic soil communities.

In the spirit and tradition of Aldo Leopold, Terry Cunningham and the other foresters at Pioneer do not manage Leo Drey's holdings with only economic objectives in mind. They weigh the need for the forest to be financially sustainable—to pay their salaries—with other values that Cunningham described as "ecological, social, and cultural." By asking what would be best for the entire ecosystem in which they live and work, the Pioneer foresters avoid what Vandana Shiva calls the "monoculture of the mind."

The uneven-age management system has gradually gained converts across the country. Auburn forestry professor Edward F. Lowenstein began his research at Pioneer with plans of disproving the viability of uneven-aged silviculture. But after an exhaustive study of all 486 research plots within the forest, he became one of Pioneer's most knowledgeable advocates. Nor is Lowenstein the only convert. The Forest Guild, a national organization, was founded on many of Pioneer's core principles. The guild defines "excellent forestry" as practices that go "beyond meeting minimum best management practices and place the long-term viability of the forest above all other considerations."

Terry Cunningham is under no illusion that Pioneer's success will put an end to clear-cutting. But the success of Pioneer *does* plainly demonstrate that a more sustainable, more responsible alternative exists. Cunningham told Jim and me at the end of our visit, "People say, 'You're comparing apples and oranges,' and that's fine with me. I don't have a problem with that. My problem is with the people who act like oranges don't exist."

This apples-only thinking was precisely the logic behind the clear-cut in Robinson Forest. The streamside management zone study, whatever its conclusions, perpetuated the attitude that there is no other way to harvest timber. That is to say, its proponents proclaimed their intent to determine the "best management practices" for clear-cutting near a stream, but they did not even consider the idea that the best management practice might be to *never* clear-cut close to a stream in the first place. When foresters at Kentucky's flagship institution assume that erosion, loss of biodiversity, and the destruction of woodlots for generations to come are simply the unavoidable costs of doing business, we have to wonder if "best management practices" *could* exist under those conditions. We should ask: *best management practices compared to what?* Clear-cutting is certainly not better than uneven-aged management, at least not where the ecosystem is concerned, particularly a unique one like Robinson Forest. There are other ways to think about forestry, ecosystems, and economics.

Consider this: the UK forestry department's website states that half of Kentucky is "commercially valuable forest land," and that 90 percent of that land resides in small, private holdings. Then it goes on to claim, "Much of the data gleaned from the wise use and experimentation at Robinson Forest ultimately provides valuable information to the private landowners for effective management of their own forested lands." But what if those private landowners don't *want* to clear-cut their woodlots? What if they don't want to look out at acres of tree stumps, but would rather make a steadier long-term profit while retaining the woodland character of their holdings? If that were the case, then the SMZ study in Robinson Forest would be of very little use to local landowners while the research that has been done at Pioneer over the last fifty years would be of profound importance.

I am not suggesting that the uneven-age model can simply be lifted from the flatlands of Missouri and used in the mountains of eastern Kentucky. It cannot. But that is all the more reason to begin research in Robinson Forest that takes the *principles* followed at Pioneer—imitating natural processes as a model of good forestry, considering ecological as well as economic values—and applying them to our own regional geography. UK's forestry department claims that its mission is to "enhanc[e] the integrity, stability, and health of forests and related biotic communities" in Kentucky. That language certainly echoes Aldo Leopold's famous definition of a *land ethic*, but it is hard to see how the SMZ study fulfilled any of Leopold's criteria. The conclusion is inescapable: *such destructive research should never again take place in Robinson Forest.*

The good news is that may very well be the case. The students who rallied against the clear-cut quite likely pulled off the classic maneuver of losing the battle but winning the war. By calling unwelcome attention to the unsustainable management practices in use in Robinson Forest, they may have ensured that such practices do not happen again. After the UK Board of Trustees approved the SMZ project, I met with forestry chair Steve Bullard, who seemed to be feeling the full sting of the opposition's rebuke. "It would be hard for me to see someone proposing something of that magnitude again," he told me, adding that any future logging research in Robinson Forest "would be around what we need to do to maintain healthy oak regeneration." If that is indeed the case, then the Pioneer Forest model has never been more relevant to the research that might go forward in central Appalachia. Bullard cited Leopold's land ethic, then elaborated: "We're uniquely positioned in Robinson Forest to showcase our vision to become regionally and nationally known, much like the Pioneer Forest. So if you envision something like a huge area to be clear-cut, I have a hard time seeing where that fits in."

Indeed, the fact that Robinson Forest is the largest remaining mixed-mesophytic ecosystem on the Cumberland Plateau *does* offer UK an opportunity to distinguish itself in terms of university stewardship, forestry management, research, and education. These contiguous four-teen thousand acres could become the premiere research forest in the Southeast—but not without some changes in how the university manages the forest. Specifically, Jim Krupa and I believe that UK must adopt a new management plan and must also expand the committee that approves research in the forest to include faculty from outside the college of agriculture.

First, the 2004 Robinson Forest Management Plant should be rewritten to better reflect a commitment to research instead of revenue. As the plan stands now, extensive timber cutting can continue in the Clemons Fork, Coles Fork, and Lewis Fork watersheds, and timber can "be cleared" throughout the rest of the forest "in rare situations." What is most troubling about the language in much of the 2004 management plan is that it conflates the laudable goals of "research and education" with a perceived need for revenue from timber harvests. Passages about research and education quickly veer into projections of a sixty- to eighty-year rotation for timber extraction. Only rarely do a university's aspirations for its research and education align with its desire for revenue, and nowhere is this more evident than in such talk of logging (or mining) in Robinson Forest. The management plan insists that logging will be done only at "harvest levels consistent with sustainable timber management calculations," and that it "must be accomplished while protecting ecosystem function, water quality and aquatic habitats, archeological and other special areas, and maintaining and improving biodiversity." But then it goes on to call for harvesting seventy acres per year "as part of research and demonstration projects."

Some serious questions arise here. What "sustainable timber management calculations" will be used to determine how much of the forest is cut? Moreover, *how* will the timber be removed? Will it simply be clear-cut, as was done in the SMZ study? How could that be called sustainable timber management? No one who has walked through that eight-hundred-acre plot would agree that the SMZ study protected ecosystem function, aquatic habitats, and biodiversity. How, therefore, will logging research be done in the future to actually meet such criteria? And in what possible scenario is research required for an annual seventy-acre clear-cut that, over the eighty-year span of its rotation, would log almost half of the remaining forest? It seems obvious that such a plan is driven almost exclusively by the desire for revenue, not by the need for research. The new management plan for Robinson Forest must be (in the language of economists) decoupled from any talk of revenue streams for the university.

Beyond the need for a new management plan, decisions about what research takes place in Robinson Forest should require final approval from a university-wide committee. Currently, the decision-making body, the Robinson Forest Technical Committee, comprises members of the UK forestry department. Jim and I maintain that this committee must be expanded to include participants from across the university—faculty members from the biological sciences, the social sciences, and the humanities. Had this been the case when the SMZ study was proposed and approved, the Technical Committee might not have been blindsided by the objections that came from within the university community and across the entire state of Kentucky. Academic disciplines, because they are made up of specialists, often breed a singular way of thinking about a subject such as Robinson Forest. Such thinking can lead to great innovation, but it can also lead to insularity, territorialism, defensiveness, and poor judgment. Decisions, for example, about the SMZ study were made without consulting Jim, a biologist who understands the streams of Robinson Forest and their aquatic communities better than anyone else. No one from the field of environmental ethics was consulted, nor were conservation organizations. Indeed, there were no letters of support for the SMZ study from anyone outside the field of forestry. And because of that, students who belonged to those organizations had no choice but to stage a sit-in at the university president's office. But it should never have come to that. Of course, if the Robinson Forest Committee had been expanded to include such points of view, the SMZ project might not have been approved in the first place—which is exactly why the committee needs to represent the broader interests of the university and of the state.

The value of Robinson Forest far exceeds the price of its timber or the information that might be gained from clear-cutting around one of the state's benchmark streams. To slowly log the forest in parcels, or to allow mining on its outlying tracts, is like killing the last passenger pigeon by plucking one feather at a time. In the end, the bird will die and the forest will be open to invasive species and silted streams. The most important forest in Kentucky will become just another industrial landscape. As with the passenger pigeon, something rare will be lost and life on the Cumberland Plateau will become less interesting. Students of the University of Kentucky and citizens of the commonwealth deserve a better legacy than that.

CHAPTER 6

Riffles and Runs and Cool, Clear Pools

James J. Krupa

Water is the lifeblood of Robinson Forest. Pumped into the forest as rain and snow, it trickles through the forest floor like blood moving through a maze of capillaries. When trees are leafed out and growing, they pull enough water to fill several reservoirs up their trunks and into their leaves, where it is transformed by photosynthesis into sugar and oxygen. Much of the water departs the leaves as vapor. Water that escapes capture by trees trickles down into the hollows and forms the headwaters of infant streams. Like veins, headwater streams merge into larger streams that increase in volume as they take on water from tributaries. This is the forest's circulatory system and a crucial part of the global water cycle. The water that escapes as vapor ends up in the atmosphere and can circulate anywhere over the planet. Water that departs the forest via streams flows into the Kentucky, Ohio, and Mississippi Rivers, then into the Gulf of Mexico and on into the oceans of the world. Eventually this water, after spending time at distant points on the globe, will return as rain and snow to feed Robinson's forest and streams.

The major watersheds of Robinson Forest are Clemons Fork to the west and Coles Fork to the east. The headwaters of Wet Fork and Carpenter Branch join the headwaters of Clemons Fork, which grows as it picks up flow from Millseat Branch, Little Millseat, Boardinghouse Branch, and Roaring Fork. Now at its greatest volume, Clemons Fork spills into Buckhorn Creek, which has already received the water from Coles Fork.

All of Robinson's flowing water leaves by way of Buckhorn Creek, which dumps into Troublesome Creek before heading to the Kentucky River.

Robinson Forest is a maze of hollows, all carved out by streams. Seams of sandstone, flint, coal, and shale are worn down as water relentlessly gnaws away; sandstone, the most resistant to erosion, persists longest. Sandstone rocks line the shores alongside streams, and the streambeds are littered with sandstone rubble of small rocks, gravel, and sand. Floods tumble these rocks downstream, and along the way they collide and chip, disintegrating into quartz sand. Eventually all stream rock is reduced to sand and carried away by the current.

The surveyors who mapped the forest gave every headwater hollow and stream a name. The history behind many of the names has been lost, although some clearly refer to past events. Some of the hollows are named for those who once lived in the forest: John Miller Hollow, Goff Hollow, and Stacy Hollow. Some are named for farm animals that lived with the landowners: Horse Hollow and Steer Hollow. Some honor the art of distillation—Gin Hollow, Rye Hollow, and Apple Hollow—while others are named for trees and mammals that live in the forest: Coon Hollow, Pawpaw Hollow, Beechnut Hollow, and Buckeye Hollow. Others are descriptive of the hollow itself: Grassy Hollow, Cool Hollow, and Stinking Hollow. Splash Hollow is named for a splash dam that existed at its mouth more than one hundred years ago. Other hollows have names that are simply intriguing. Who died in Deadman's Hollow? Who committed suicide in Suicide Hollow? Sometimes the survey crew named a headwater stream but not the hollow: Panther Fork, Bee Creek, Tom Branch, and Bracken Branch. Some streams are named for plants, especially trees—Big Laurel Branch, White Oak Fork—and others are geographically descriptive: Grassy Gap Branch, Ridge Fork, Long Branch, and Falling Rock Branch. Improvement Branch suggests a major landscaping event. Boardinghouse Branch, a seasonal stream flowing through Camp Robinson into Clemons Fork, is named for Mowbray and Robinson's boardinghouse, now demolished, where loggers once lived.

Robinson's three largest streams (Clemons Fork, Coles Fork, and Buckhorn Creek) are a study in contrast. The substrates of each are markedly different. Coles Fork tends to be sandier, while Clemons Fork is rockier and littered with pieces of flint found in none of the other streams. Buckhorn Creek is the widest of the three, and because it flows through reclaimed surface mines before entering Robinson Forest, it carries a heavy load of silt. Many stream ecologists say that Clemons Fork and Coles Fork are two of the cleanest streams in Kentucky. Others say they are the cleanest in the eastern coalfields.

Like Clemons Fork, Coles Fork has experienced major human disturbance from road and railroad construction, damming, clear-cutting, and destructive logging practices. After recent floods, Coles Fork no longer has a functional road. Much of the road paralleled the stream, and occasionally crossed it. Along some stretches, the stream was the road. With the road now washed out, Coles Fork looks much as it did two hundred years ago, before European settlers arrived. And for the first time in two hundred years, Coles Fork is close to being pristine again, although only close because nonnative plants are probably present. This recovery is testimony to Coles Fork's resilience.

Walking the length of Coles Fork gives the impression that it is a drainage system that humanity and time have forgotten. Azaleas and mountain laurels, normally small to mid-sized shrubs, grow like trees. Dense stands of eastern hemlocks tower over the stream. Rosebay rhododendrons with their dark, glossy evergreen leaves are larger here than elsewhere in the forest, their dense branches nearly impenetrable. The absence of motorized vehicles, trash, and other evidence of recent human activity engenders a serene feeling of being in wilderness despite mountaintop removal occurring less than a mile away.

A distinct community of plants thrives in the rich, moist soils along the shores of Robinson's streams. Eastern hemlocks, umbrella magnolias, sycamores, and willows, along with American and slippery elms, form a canopy that provides cooling shade for the shrubs that thrive in the understory. Hazel-alders form tall thickets along the stream banks at the water's edge. Yellow-flowered witch hazels bloom from October to November on slightly higher ground, along with spicebush, which sports bright red autumn berries. Horsetails and many ferns (sensitive fern, glade fern, wood fern, and silvery glade fern) are rarely found far from streams, and many small flowering plants are most abundant on the moist, rich banks. Partridgeberry, foamflower, jack-in-the pulpit, and red trillium thrive. Mixed with them are blue phlox, great lobelia, mistflower, jewelweed, goat's beard, dwarf crested iris, and a host of violets, especially marsh violets.

Stands of Indian pipe can sometimes be found above the flood line. These small, parasitic white plants lack chlorophyll and are thus unable to photosynthesize. With the help of fungal associates they rob nutrients from the roots of other plants. Liverworts, iridescent green plants that lack flowers, leaves, stems, and roots, often cover large pieces of sandstone along the shore, their small, leathery bodies like green scales blanketing the rocks.

Many animals depend on Robinson's streams. Water striders—insects with long, oarlike legs—skate over the water hunting small insects trapped on the surface. Crayfish crawl over stream bottoms looking for detritus to eat. They forage by night to avoid predatory fish and scoot under the flat rocks scattered about the stream bottom when threatened. Flat pieces of sandstone resting partially submerged along the shore provide refuge for salamanders. Two-lined salamanders are common, their internal organs visible through their thin, transparent yellow bellies. One can count a gravid female's eggs right through the skin. Seal salamanders and dusky salamanders, small, dark gray–and-brown creatures, also live under shoreline rocks. Pickerel frogs sit motionless along the shore waiting to capture anything that moves and can be swallowed. Frogs have a very simple outlook on life: if it moves and fits in your mouth, eat it. If it moves and is too big to fit in your mouth (but not big enough to eat you), mate with it. Like all frogs, the pickerel's tongue is hinged at the front of the mouth so it can be flipped out at prey. The frog captures and brings in its prey—even a fast-skating water strider—with one quick flick of the long, sticky tongue. The pickerel frogs' backs have large, square blotches separated by greenish-yellow skin that help the frogs blend perfectly with the shore. They are rarely seen until disturbed; then they leap into the stream with a flash of their bright yellow underside. It is suggested that this flash coloration momentarily disorients a predator. By the time the predator regains its focus, the pickerel frog is resting on the bottom of the stream, once again camouflaged against its surroundings.

Measured by biomass and species diversity, fish are the dominant group of animals in Robinson's streams. Most of Robinson's fish belong to four families: twelve species of the minnow family (Cyprinidae), eight species of darters belonging to the perch family (Percidae), seven species of sunfish and bass of the sunfish family (Centrachidae), and three species of the sucker family (Catistomidae). Many of these species exhibit extreme sexual dimorphism resulting from the driving evolutionary force of sexual selection. Males compete with each other for the right to mate with females, and females choose males with the attributes most appealing to them. Consequently, males tend to be more brightly colored and ornamented than females (like the peacock's tail, the male cardinal's red feathers, and the bull elk's antlers), although few visitors to Robinson Forest ever witness this.

Clemons and Cole Forks and the Buckhorn seem too small and shallow to host thirty-two species of fish. Among the reasons for the species diversity is the streams' physical complexity: each stream comprises a series of riffles, runs, and pools. Riffles drop off at an angle steeper than other parts of a stream. They are filled with rocks over which water flows quickly and look like miniature rapids. Runs are flat, wide, and shallow. Water flows slowly and silently over a run. Pools are deep and clear, often adjacent to large blocks of sandstone resting on the stream bank or large sycamore trees with a tangle of roots beneath the water's surface.

Each of these zones is a distinct habitat that some aquatic organisms prefer and others avoid. Fish adapted for living in riffles and adept at fighting the fast currents, for example, do not do well in deep pools. Fish adapted to maneuver through the water column of a pool do poorly in the shallow, fast water of a riffle. Both riffle- and pool-loving fish do venture into runs, where they mingle with schools of long-bodied, streamlined fish that can swim at great speeds though the open, shallow water. Riffles, runs, and pools create a complex ecosystem that favors biodiversity.

Sunfish and bass lurk in deep, placid pools, feeding on small fish, snails, crayfish, and any insect trapped on the water's surface. The smallmouth bass, a big fish that lives in small pools, is a "sit and wait" predator that hides in submerged tangles of sycamore roots and shoots out like an arrow to ambush its prey. Other predatory sunfish—spotted bass, green sunfish, long-eared sunfish, and rock bass—lurk in deep pools as well, making these dangerous places that small fish had best avoid. Smallmouth bass and rock bass are particularly fond of crayfish; oddly, both bass have bright red eyes. Pools with smallmouth bass and rock bass are usually devoid of crayfish. Sunfish and bass are very agile. Their wide, flexible fins, especially the pectoral fins, move the fish up and down through the water column smoothly and gracefully. They can move forward and backward slowly or quickly, and can cut right or left in an instant. They can hover in place and then disappear with a sudden burst of speed. Their agility and maneuverability make them imposing predators.

Male bass in Robinson's Forest are not brightly colored, and most adult male sunfish have only a yellow-and-orange breast and belly to entice females. The exception is the male long-eared sunfish, which display multiple shades of orange, blue, and green. The fins are orange. The belly is bright yellow and covered with dark orange spots, and iridescent blue spots cover the dark orange back. Blue vermiculations, or worm lines, accentuate the head. The large black opercular flap is edged with a white border that extends backward from the gill, giving the long-eared sunfish its name.

Minnows dominate the runs. During the spring breeding season, males of many species develop stunning coloration. Rosefin shiners have red fins and a blue body. Rosyface shiners have a bright red head. Male striped shiners sport shimmering pink scales and dark pink fins. Male stonerollers have orange fins, an orange-yellow belly, and a mottled brown back flecked with deep orange. The blacknosed dace, which has a translucent, blood red lateral band running the length of the body over black and brown blotches, is the rarest of Robinson's minnows. The silver-jawed minnow has shiny silver sides, each scale like a mirror. Male spotfin shiners and bluntnose minnows lack flashy breeding colors, but their head becomes dark, almost black. Minnows have a strong proclivity to school much of the year, with as many as eight species mingling together. In the spring, these swirling schools flash silver, red, pink, orange, and blue.

Stonerollers play a significant role in a stream's ecology. They are algae-eating grazers, the ichthyological equivalent of sheep and cattle. When stonerollers are missing from a stream, a layer of green algae covers the bed. When they are present, the rocks show their true colors of yellow, orange, and brown. Male stonerollers are much larger than females and look like fish on steroids. The body is thick and muscular, and the disproportionately large head sports an abundance of horny, toothlike tubercles. Like the antlers of a bull elk, these are used for combat and display. As the name implies, male stonerollers roll stones. When the mating season nears, males stake out their nest sites in depressions they form in runs. Powered by muscle, determination, and the current, the male stoneroller uses his head to roll gravel and small rocks downstream from the depression, creating a pile that looks like miniature mine tailings. Once nest construction is completed, the male swims over the nest, displaying his magnificent orange coloration and the impressive tubercles that signal his sexual prowess and superiority. When a female arrives, the male swims up alongside her, releasing his sperm as she releases her eggs. The sticky fertilized eggs sink to the bottom of the nest and attach to gravel. The female departs, leaving the male behind to guard the eggs and try to attract more mates. Other breeding minnows use stoneroller nests as well, swarming above them in frenzied orgies, dumping their eggs and sperm. The eggs settle into the stoneroller's nest and gravel tailing, where they develop. The male stoneroller is left guarding his eggs as well as those of other minnows.

As beautiful as Robinson's breeding minnows are, they pale in comparison with the spectacular colors of male darters, small fish that prefer riffles and to a lesser extent runs. Adults range in length from one to five inches depending on the species. Because they lack a swim bladder, darters have great difficulty swimming up through the water column. They spend most of their lives bouncing along riffles and runs, swimming short distances in quick bursts, darting—as their name implies— from rock to rock. Darters are visually oriented fish that can survive only in clear, clean, cool water. Males compete with each other for the best rocks, the ones with crevices and ledges where females can lay their eggs. Females prefer the flashiest males of proven quality. The more brilliantly colored the male, the more likely a female will select his rock as the location to deposit her eggs.

Greenside darters are the largest, reaching five inches in length. During the breeding season the male's body is saturated with multiple shades of green: the head and most fins become deep green; the dorsal fins are banded with orange and green; and thick, vertical green bands run the length of the body. Tiny orange spots are scattered over the top half of the body. The much smaller emerald darter has iridescent emerald green bands that seem to glow and a dorsal fin banded with orange and green stripes.

The rainbow darter has a fitting name. Its fins are red, orange, and blue. The head and anterior body are deep blue, and the rest of the body has alternating blue and orange bands. Male variegated darters are yet another standout. The head is blue-gray, the belly is a blazing orange that extends halfway up the body, and the rest of the body is banded blue and orange. The fins range from solid blue to solid orange, some having stripes of blue and orange.

Not all of Robinson Forest's darters are brilliantly colored despite being sexually dimorphic. Johnny darters are tiny, straw yellow fish marked on the sides with small black xs and ws. During the breeding season, the male's head and fins turn black and the body darkens. Johnny darters may not be as flashy as the others, but their black body is striking nonetheless. The black-sided darter is the least colorful and least sexually dimorphic of the group. It has a straw yellow belly and pale olive back. The body is saddled and blotched with large patches of black.

The fantail darter is the oddest of the group. Males are not particularly flashy; breeding males develop a black head and pale yellow-orange body. Yet they have something no other fish in Robinson has. At the tip of each ray on the anterior dorsal fin is a translucent orange-yellow sphere the size, shape, and color of a fantail egg. Breeding male darters seek out and defend rocks with horizontal crevices, where they display in hope of convincing females to mate with them. If the male is successful, the female will attach her eggs to the crevice ceiling. Besides displaying their brilliant colors, male darters convince females they are worthy mates by showing that other females have already laid eggs on the rock. "Other females chose me," they seem to advertise, "and so should you!" Male fantails go a step further than other fantails and resort to trickery. They press the egglike spheres on their dorsal fin against the ceiling to falsely advertise a previous female's attraction. Apparently it works.

When I arrived in Kentucky in 1989, I was most excited by the state's tremendous fish biodiversity. More than two hundred species live in Kentucky's vast stream systems, and I wanted to see them all. The reason I first visited Robinson Forest in 1991 was to see one species in particular, the Kentucky arrow darter, the crown jewel of Robinson's collection of magnificent fish. The name describes their shape when young: long and thin bodied with an extremely pointed head. They have a unique "double dot" marking at the base of the tail like a colon punctuating the end of the fish. When in peak color, the male arrow darter is spectacular, with blue-streaked black pelvic fins, a deep blue anal fin, and clear yellow pectoral fins on a blue-green body scattered with scarlet dots, each with a yellow halo. Three horizontal bands of color ornament the anterior dorsal fin, blue-green below yellow and orange. The posterior dorsal fin is yellow and blue with rows of orange spots. The tail is yellow with rows of orange dots with a blue band at its base, and the belly is a brilliant mix of yellow and orange that looks like a miniature sunset.

Many of North America's darters are endangered or at risk of becoming endangered, threatened by global warming, water pollution, and turbidity from runoff. The Kentucky arrow darter, never very common, is among them. It is becoming increasingly rare in part because of its limited distribution. It lives in the streams of only six counties on the Cumberland Plateau in Kentucky and Tennessee. The eastern coalfields are this fish's home, and any fish associated with coal beds is a species in trouble. Mountaintop removal is accelerating the arrow darter's decline. When the tops of mountains are pushed as overburden down into the hollows, the arrow darter's habitat is destroyed. The darters seem to be holding on in a few streams in Kentucky and Tennessee, and for now, Clemons and Cole Forks provide sanctuary.

The largest fish in the streams of Robinson Forest, the suckers, prefer to live in runs, where they rest on the streambed below schools of minnows. They are long-bodied, torpedo-shaped bottom feeders with a fleshy-lipped mouth that protrudes downward from the bottom of the head. The toothless, round mouth is perfectly shaped for vacuuming aquatic creatures out from under rocks and from the spaces between pieces of gravel. Two species, white suckers and northern hog suckers, are solitary bottom feeders that prefer to move slowly, feeding as they go. Their coloration matches the streambed, and thus they are rarely seen. White suckers rest on rock rubble, the hydrodynamic body pointed upstream to minimize drag from flowing water, invisible until they are disturbed. Stepping too close to one in a stream can trigger the sucker's escape response. They are powerful swimmers that show tremendous speed when threatened, and large individuals can swim against the current with enough force to leave a wake. Once it feels safe, the white sucker stops and again blends into its background.

Northern hogsuckers are an exaggeration of the basic sucker body plan. Their eyes are located on a column of bone that protrudes disturbingly from the sides of the head. The mouth is orange and exceedingly long and fleshy, extending well below the head like the nozzle of a vacuum cleaner attachment. The back is mottled black, gray, and brown, and the sides are banded black and orange. The pectoral and pelvic fins are orange and blend surprisingly well with sandstone gravel. When caught they seem bewildered, issuing subtle grunts to signal their confused protest. I find their appearance hideous to the point of being oddly beautiful, and I cannot help but laugh every time I catch one. Everything about a hogsucker is humorous.

The golden redhorse is a sucker too, but very different from its two camouflaged and solitary cousins. It is a social fish fond of swimming long distances. Nomadic schools of up to fifty sleek, shiny, flat-sided golden redhorse cruise up and down the Buckhorn. The dorsal fin and tail are black, and the other fins range from orange to yellow. These are large (more than a foot long), streamlined, fast-swimming fish covered with large, silvery scales. The water sparkles and glistens when a big school of golden redhorse races up the Buckhorn.

The most common fish in Robinson Forest is the creek chub, a large minnow found in streams of all sizes. Often they are the only fish in headwaters. Big creek chubs like deep pools, where they live alongside smallmouth bass and rock bass in root tangles. They eat any aquatic animal they encounter, including smaller fish. While sunfish and bass have the toothy jaws expected of a predator, the creek chub has a big mouth with no teeth. Despite this, they are formidable predators. They have toothlike structures called pharyngeal teeth attached to the gill arches deep in the throat. The pharyngeal teeth are larger than the teeth of a smallmouth bass and hold prey tightly until the fish swallows it.

Fish biologists who teach ichthyology in the Midwest can always find teachable moments (i.e., pranks to inflict on students). Catching an especially large creek chub is such an opportunity. When I was a graduate student taking ichthyology in western Nebraska, our class netted a huge creek chub one afternoon. We stood around the bucket in which the chub swam while the professor lectured on the form and function of pharyngeal teeth. He was a rather obnoxious character who often pulled pranks on his students, but it was the first week of class and I had yet to discover that. He told us that placing a pinky finger down the throat of a creek chub was the best way to feel how firmly pharyngeal teeth clamp down and asked for a volunteer to demonstrate it. I quickly stepped forward. The chub was a monster of its species, being nearly twelve inches long with a mouth big enough to engulf my finger. I poked my finger down the fish's throat. Nothing happened. Then the fish clamped down with more force than I anticipated. It did not hurt, but it was a shock, and I let out a shriek as the fish dropped back into the stream and swam away. My classmates laughed. I stood red-faced in the stream and imagined pulling this prank on my own students someday.

The day finally arrived twenty years later when my vertebrate biology class was spending the weekend in Robinson Forest. We caught a ten-inch creek chub in Buckhorn Creek, and I launched into an impromptu lecture on the form and function of pharyngeal teeth. I asked for a volunteer to provide a finger for demonstration. No one stepped forward. We were in the tenth week of the semester, and my students had long ago figured me out. So I stuck my own finger down the creek chub's throat. What I learned in Buckhorn Creek that day was that the pharyngeal teeth of creek chubs may not be sharp in Nebraska streams, but they are like needles in Robinson Forest. The creek chub clamped down, and I let out a loud yelp. The fish dropped into the stream and swam away, leaving me standing there with blood streaming from two very pronounced puncture wounds in my finger. My students were horrified that I had been willing to inflict such pain on them and refused to believe my protests that I hadn't known the teeth were so sharp.

The most ancient, and perhaps the oddest, of Robinson's fish is confined to the sand and silt beds along the lower reaches of Coles Fork. The American brook lamprey is a member of a class of fish known as the Agnatha (jawless fish), the first vertebrate animals to appear on earth 500 million years ago. Everything about a lamprey looks primitive and ancient. They are very long and skinny with a slimy body that is impossible to grip. Dark gray in color, lampreys look like foot-long aquatic worms. The skeleton is made of flexible cartilage rather than calcified bone as is the case for most vertebrates. They lack a lower jaw, an essential tool for any predator. Adult lampreys have a suction-cup mouth filled with teeth. Many species of lampreys are parasites that feed on large fish, often without killing them. The lamprey attaches its mouth to the side of the fish and uses its sharp rasping teeth to gnaw into the body of the victim, consuming tissue and fluids. The best-known parasitic lamprey, the sea lamprey, invaded the Great Lakes in the 1940s and wiped out commercially important lake trout and whitefish populations. Robinson Forest's lamprey is neither parasitic nor destructive. It spends the first five or six years of its life as a larva buried in mud, silt, and sand with only its head protruding into the water. The larva has no teeth and is a filter feeder. It sucks water into its mouth, extracts small animals and detritus, which it swallows, then expels the filtered water out its gills.

Eventually the larva metamorphoses into an adult with a suction-cup mouth full of small teeth. The teeth are not needed because the adult will never eat. The digestive tract degenerates while the reproductive organs swell. American brook lampreys are nothing more than swimming testes and ovaries that enter into a spawning frenzy in early spring and then die. It is rare to see adults; one needs to be in Coles Fork at the right time in spring. I have waded Coles Fork on cool April days to see adult lampreys by the hundreds swirling about, releasing clouds of eggs and sperm to start the next generation. The orgy lasts a few days and then the exhausted lampreys die. I have never found a lamprey in Clemons Fork or in the Buckhorn. The Buckhorn may become better habitat for these odd fish as it continues to silt over, but lampreys prefer cleaner water that the Buckhorn may not be able to provide. Time will tell.

Robinson's stream dwellers face diverse types of predators. They come in many forms, including larger fish, spiders, reptiles, birds, and mammals. They attack from the water below, the surface, the shore, and overhanging tree branches. The smallest and youngest fish face a great crush of predation from multiple directions. When they hug the shorelines to avoid being eaten by other fish, they risk death from fishing spiders. With legs spread, the largest fishing spiders almost cover the palm of my hand. They hunt the shorelines day and night, perching motionless at the stream's edge with front legs resting gently atop the water. They can detect the slightest motion made by fish, salamanders, or water striders. In an instant and without warning they attack, pulling fish and amphibians out of the water and plucking water striders off the surface. The first adult fishing spider I ever saw in Robinson Forest was a shock. I flipped over a rock and saw the long tail of a dusky salamander protruding from a crevice. Assuming it was trying to escape from me, I gently pulled the salamander out by the tail, only then realizing that a fishing spider was holding on to the other end. The salamander was dead and decapitated; the spider had been devouring it head-first. I am very familiar with fishing spiders, having been around them years, yet to this day, unexpectedly coming on an adult sunning along the shoreline gives me a jolt.

Larger fish have their predators as well. Northern water snakes hunt underwater, probing their head under rocks and into crevices. They slide into root tangles and undercut banks in search of fish. These snakes have many sharp teeth that help grip slimy fish as they are swallowed whole. Raccoons patrol the shorelines and shallows, trapping fish in crevices and capturing salamanders and crayfish hiding under rocks. Mink, agile swimmers, are capable of diving into deep pools and capturing medium-sized and large fish. The largest fish have little to fear from snakes and raccoons but must be vigilant nonetheless, for if they venture into the open, great blue herons will spear them from above.

Belted kingfishers patrol streams year-round searching for fish. They are strikingly beautiful birds with deep blue feathers covering the head, back, and tops of the wings, which are accented in black and white. A scruffy blue crest adorns the top of the head like a bad hairdo in need of combing. The robust black beak is long and sharp—perfect for spearing fish. When hunting, a kingfisher perches motionless on a tree branch above the stream waiting for fish to wander out into open water. The aerial attack is sudden and without warning. The kingfisher drops from the branch, momentarily hovers over its intended prey, and then the plunge dive. In a flash, a streak of black is followed by a blur of blue as the kingfisher slices through the water and spears the fish. When not perched looking for prey, kingfishers are raucous and in perpetual motion, racing up and down streams, constantly scolding, always heard before they are seen. A slight flash of blue in the distance, and suddenly this powerful bird, propelled by pulsing blue wings with flashing white crescents, rockets overhead and is gone.

Robinson Forest's streams are ever in flux, constantly changing from season to season, year to year, and decade to decade. Logging, splash dams, road construction, violent flash floods, and fires have drastically altered the streams, yet given time they are capable of recovering from significant disturbance. Droughts and heat waves can reduce streams to trickles, killing much of the life that depends on flowing water. There are hard years that push life to its limits and good years when aquatic life explodes in abundance. In good years there are no floods, no droughts, no heat waves, and abundant rain falls evenly through spring, summer, and fall. These are the years when stream life recovers.

Streams flow steadily and at their greatest volume during the winter. This is a good time for fish. The deeper water protects them from raccoons, mink, and kingfishers. Water snakes are dormant and pose no threat. Food is more abundant, giving young fish the opportunity to grow quickly and giving adult fish time to build up energy reserves for the breeding season.

The winter wren is a tiny migratory bird that resides along Robinson's streams when the summer residents have gone south for the winter. Its wings are tiny and rounded, and its short tail points upward. These hyperactive little brown-and-gray birds blend into the drab winter shoreline as they flit and fly and hop along the stream banks, probing into cracks and crevices, under leaf litter and overhanging moss, incessantly searching for food. It is hard to get a good look at one—most often all one sees is a brief flash of gray. When disturbed, winter wrens appear seemingly from nowhere, popping up from the stream bank, flying a short distance downstream, only to disappear again. As the days of March grow longer and the air grows warmer, winter wrens get the urge to begin the migration back to their breeding grounds in Canada.

The departure of the winter wren means that spring is imminent, but the departure of a small gray bird is not the signal of spring that most people notice. The arrival of color is a signal that cannot be overlooked. On the tail of the wren's departure arrives the most magnificent of all North American ducks. Wood ducks appear along Buckhorn Creek in early spring. With respect to color, they are the long-eared sunfish of the bird world. Male wood ducks are iridescent and multicolored. The green head has a swept-back crest more exaggerated than that of females. They have a white chin, white stripes on the head, and a rusty red breast, and white and black bands separate the breast from the yellow-tan sides. The much more subdued females are a mix of brown and light gray with a drab, swept-back crest that looks like the ducktail hairstyle of the 1950s. These are perching ducks; that is, they sit on tree branches and nest in tree cavities. They prefer cavities close to streams so that on the day of hatching, ducklings tumble out of the cavity and drop directly into the water. The next best option is for these little fuzzballs to fall into soft leaf litter followed by a quick scramble to the stream.

The arrival of wood ducks is a signal that spring flowers will soon bloom along the stream banks. The spring pageant of color comes in waves. The first wave of flowers to appear along the streams includes hepatica, bloodroot, rue anemone, spring beauty, harbinger-of-spring, cutleaf toothwort, early saxifrage, and colt's foot. Soon the second wave arrives with an even greater show of color: blue phlox, Virginia bluebell, Jacob's ladder, golden ragwort, dwarf larkspur, buttercup, early meadow rue, wood anemone, celandine poppy, Dutchman's breeches, chickweed, baneberry, sweet Cicely, yellow pimpernel, wood sorrel, bluets, green violets, foamflower, jack-in-the-pulpit, and red trillium. At the trailing edge of this second wave, wild geranium, mayapple, thimbleweed, fire pink, columbine, Carolina vetch, and goat's beard begin to bloom. In the third and final wave of late spring are tall meadow rue, black cohosh, whorled loosestrife, honewort, ginseng, daisy fleabane, jewelweed, waterleaf, meehania, skullcap, houstonia, partridgeberry, and alumroot.

As the pageant of flowers covers the stream banks, waves of color appear in and above the stream as well. Minnows and darts erupt into their breeding colors. Migratory warblers filter through the canopy, home from the south, some from as far away as South America. These are the darters of the bird world with names that signify their dazzling array of colors: blue-winged, orange-crowned, chestnut-sided, black-throated blue, black-throated green, redstart, blackburnian, yellow-rumped, yellow-throated, golden-winged, bay-breasted, cerulean, and black-and-white. Many other beautifully colored warblers without color in their names arrive as well: northern parula, palm, hooded, Wilson's, Kentucky, Nashville, and Tennessee.

Most of these little beauties spend their time in the canopy; however, two of the warblers are ground dwellers with drab coloration that allows them to blend into the shoreline. Waterthrushes, warblers despite their name, fill the niche left open by the departure of winter wrens. They forage along the shorelines for spiders, insects, and larvae as well as snails and small fish. Males and females alike are brown above with a light-colored breast streaked with brown. Unlike most passerine birds, waterthrushes walk rather than hop, bobbing up and down as if bouncing on springs. It seems odd that an inconspicuously colored ground-dwelling bird draws attention to itself by bobbing, yet birds all around the world that live in the same streamside niche do the same thing. There must be some adaptive advantage associated with this bobbing behavior, but I don't know what it is. Northern waterthrushes arrive in mid-spring and stay for a short time before continuing on to their breeding grounds in northern Canada. As the northerns begin their departure, the Louisiana waterthrushes arrive, easily distinguishable by their bright pink legs. Louisiana waterthrushes stay for the summer; Robinson Forest is their breeding ground.

With spring rains come spring floods. Rarely does a year go by that Robinson's streams do not suddenly transform from clear, shallow trickles to turbid, raging torrents. Clemons Fork, Coles Fork, and Buckhorn

Creek spill over their banks every spring after heavy rain, flooding the roads for a few days. After each flood, quartz sand that was once part of the Appalachian Mountains is mounded up along the shores of Buckhorn Creek. Some stretches of Buckhorn Road are annually buried by sand. In my early days at the forest, severe flooding washed out the old bridges made of concrete rubble piled atop corrugated metal pipes. The modern concrete bridges stand up to flooding but disappear under the raging torrents until the floodwaters pass.

The risk of annual spring floods is always on my mind when I take classes to the forest in April. I rarely sleep well in Camp Robinson on these trips because I am always listening for rain. The sound of hard, sustained rain hitting the roof of my cabin keeps me anxious and awake, and I have several times cut class trips short because of it. Experiencing floods in Robinson Forest has helped me understand stream behavior and flood patterns. Too many times I have stood on the banks of Clemons Fork waiting for first light on a Sunday morning, only to see the stream gray, churning, and racing by at a frightening speed. If Clemons Fork looks bad, Coles Fork will look worse, because it is a larger watershed. The problem is not these two streams themselves, but the volume they send into Buckhorn Creek and the subsequent flooding of Buckhorn Road. Of even greater concern is Troublesome Creek's transformation once the Buckhorn dumps into it. Shallow flooding on Buckhorn Road is safe to drive through, but it is a signal that Troublesome has transformed into a dangerous monster capable of engulfing the blacktop (Highway 476) and blocking our escape to Highway 15. Normally, Troublesome Creek is at least fifteen feet below the highway, with very steep banks between road and water. If Troublesome is up to the blacktop, vehicles and road alike can be washed away.

On those problematic Sunday mornings, once I've had a look at Clemons Fork I drive down the road to assess Buckhorn Creek. More than once I have found myself standing on the road knee-deep in swirling water. When this happens, I know that we have a narrow window of a few hours to get out of camp before Troublesome spills over the blacktop. Troublesome Creek truly deserves its name. I hurry back to Camp Robinson and pile students and equipment into vehicles for a hasty departure. Once one of Buckhorn's bridges went out early and my caravan of five fifteen-passenger vans and one Suburban had to snake its way up Lewis Fork Road onto reclaimed surface mines to reach the blacktop. Troublesome spilled over its banks a few hours later.

On another occasion, an especially severe thunderstorm passed farther south, and Troublesome flooded first, causing the Buckhorn to back up and flood the road. By then the blacktop was already underwater. More rain was coming, with predictions that the middle fork of the Kentucky River would flood Highway 15 by early evening. We were facing the prospect of being stranded in Camp Robinson for an extended period if we did not get out soon. The water on Buckhorn Road was steadily rising and too deep for small vehicles, so we left our two small pickup trucks at Camp Robinson and loaded everyone into the five big vans. I waded down the flooded road ahead of the caravan of vans, making sure the road was solid. Once we reached Laurel Fork Road we were driving on active surface mines as we made our escape. We reached Highway 15 and got out before the Kentucky River's middle fork flooded it that evening. So I am always on edge taking classes to Robinson Forest in the spring.

Rainstorms and flooding may inconvenience me and my students, but they are part of Robinson's ecology. I have no idea what the fish, salamanders, and water snakes do during a flood, but when the floodwaters subside, they are all still there. Flooding is part of life, and life has adapted to it.

Occasionally, floods occur that are so violent and extensive that life near the streams takes a beating, as happened in May 2009. A downpour fell fast and hard without letting up. Flash flooding hit both the Coles Fork and Clemons Fork watersheds. Camp Robinson was underwater, with some buildings sustaining structural damage. The following March 2010, I hiked the length of Coles Fork to see the extent of the damage. I know this stream well, having walked it many times, but I did not recognize the shoreline or see the landmarks I had used for twenty years. Mounds of sand were piled where there was once a road. Trees were stacked like kindling in massive piles on top of the stream. Pools where amphibians once bred were either buried by mud or scraped away, and every tadpole and larva that had been in them likely died. Many fish died as well.

What hurt me most was the realization that every female four-toed salamander along Coles Fork died along with the eggs she was guarding. Over the years I have mapped out every pool where this salamander breeds along Coles Fork. I intentionally reshaped many of the pools to improve their quality as breeding sites. I suspended moss-covered logs over pools. I positioned other mossy logs along the edge of each pool. I placed the largest sandstone rocks I could carry along the edge as well. I added a layer of soil and large pads of moss on top of them, hoping the moss would grow and provide nest sites when it blanketed the rock. In 2008 four-toed salamanders were abundant, with many females nesting around my improved breeding pools, but in March 2010 not one pool remained. The moss-covered rocks and logs were gone, and I could not find one four-toed salamander. The flood hit just when the females were guarding their eggs, so two generations of salamanders were lost. I could only hope that some nonbreeding one-year-olds were up on the slopes, safe from the flood beneath the leaf litter. I try to remember that flash floods have swept through the hollows of Robinson Forest for as long as there have been hollows. They are destructive natural events from which nature always recovers. Resiliency is part of the forest's ecology. Eventually there will again be female four-toed salamanders guarding their eggs next to pools along Coles Fork.

Violent and destructive flash flooding is a rare event. Summer droughts, on the other hand, are more frequent, more subtle, and in the end more deadly. As summer progresses, trees photosynthesize and grow, sucking up the forest's water reserves. Meanwhile, precipitation declines and heat rises. Water evaporates from the forest more rapidly. Stream flow slows, and water levels drop. In a typical year, riffles shrink, runs become trickles, and the remaining pools become refuges for all of the fish.

In a dry year, fish are in a battle to survive, and their struggle for existence is painful to witness. Many die. Clemons and Coles Forks transform into small, isolated pools. If the drought persists, many pools shrink to puddles. By September the situation is dire. Fish compete with each other for limited food. Fry from the spring hatch are the first to die. Big predatory fish devour little fish and in turn become prey themselves. With riffles and runs dry, darters are forced to hide under rocks in pools. Suckers tuck themselves under rock shelves in the deepest pools. The phrase "like shooting fish in a barrel" becomes harsh reality. Water snakes gorge themselves on minnows that cannot escape. Mink and raccoons feast on fish and salamanders. Kingfishers have their pick. As pools shrink, the slaughter accelerates until fish numbers are decimated. Water snakes find refuge and live off their newly acquired fat reserves, while the mink and raccoons head into the forest searching for other prey. The kingfisher is left to search desperately for the few remaining fish.

Every dry summer I spend at Robinson Forest I am convinced no fish will survive, but always a few pools persist. Salvation arrives in October as falling leaves fill the pools and provide protection from predators. Enough insects get trapped on the water's surface to provide food. As fall progresses, trees enter dormancy and the water they no longer absorb is diverted back into the streams. Flow increases. With late November rains, streams resume steady flow and water volume returns to normal. The surviving crayfish, salamanders, and fish reappear in numbers that exceed expectation. These survivors persist by luck or because they have some genetic attribute that helped them to survive; they will pass their adaptations to the next generation that will have to face future droughts.

Waterthrush survive the difficult summer. Adult wood ducks survive as well, although their young may be less fortunate. As fall progresses, waterthrush begin their southern migration; then the wood ducks leave. Soon winter wrens return to forage alongside healthy, flowing streams.

Nature inflicts destruction and hardship on Robinson's streams, but the worst destruction caused by nature pales in comparison with what humans have done. Someone hiking along Coles Fork today will find little evidence of the most destructive period Robinson's streams faced. Just downstream from where Ridge Branch flows into Coles Fork, a straight oak beam ten inches wide and thirty feet long extends from shore to shore beneath the streambed. It is odd to see such a large piece of wood buried in rock rubble underwater. At first glance, it appears to be the remains of a fallen tree, but closer examination shows that it is a long length of cut oak. The waters of Coles Fork have been flowing over this oak beam for more than one hundred years. It is one of the last existing signs of the massive environmental degradation that befell Robinson's streams between 1880 and 1920.

Commercial logging began in the woods that would eventually become Robinson Forest in the late 1880s. The early operations lacked the resources to build roads or the thin-railed tracks known as T-rails for transporting logs. Early loggers were creative and resourceful, though. They built six splash dams in the Coles Fork drainage. These dams, made of oak, were erected at strategic points, and reservoirs were allowed to fill behind each. Logs were either pushed down the slopes and into the reservoirs or stacked along stream banks below the dams. The loggers selected trees with lightweight wood because they floated better than the heavier oaks and hickories; as a result, eastern hemlocks, cucumbertrees, and tulip poplars were the first trees removed. During winter and spring, when water levels were at their highest volume, the splash dams were dynamited in succession, starting with the one farthest upstream. As each dam was destroyed, a tidal wave of wood and water surged downstream. Loggers would push logs into the stream as the water rushed by. When the surging water reached the next reservoir, its splash dam was dynamited. In this way, logs traveled out of Coles Fork, into the Buckhorn, and then on to Troublesome Creek where sawmills awaited. The use of splash dams caused extensive environmental damage, and not just to the forest. Farmers downstream lost their fields and occasionally barns and other outbuildings to the floodwaters. Anger and demands for compensation increased until the practice was stopped in 1912.

That was when F. W. Mowbray and E. O. Robinson arrived with the resources to run a large-scale logging operation. They built logging roads and T-rail tracks along the streams and constructed tram rails up into the small hollows. Carts pulled by oxen, mules, or gravity carried logs off the slopes and ridges. Oxen dragged individual logs directly down the slopes as well. With their more advanced technology, Mowbray and Robinson were able to remove the heavy oaks and hickories that the earlier loggers had left behind. White oaks were especially desirable to fill the growing demand for whisky and bourbon barrels. Soil erosion was extensive during this time, and much of the forest topsoil ended up as sediment in the streams. The stream ecosystem was turned upside down.

By 1922 Mowbray and Robinson had logged all the trees they wanted from the forest, leaving species they deemed undesirable standing. The streams were left in ruins. The metal from the rails was removed and sold as scrap. Ninety years later, Coles Fork has recovered. It is as close to pristine as any stream on the Cumberland Plateau can be. In fact, it looks like a stream that has never experienced human disturbance. Every now and again, as I wade up Coles Fork or Buckhorn Creek, I will find a small, rusted length of T-rail or a bent and rusted rail spike from the Mowbray and Robinson days, or the remains of a splash dam that has survived since a time before their operation ever set foot in the forest. Oak crossties still turn up in some of the hollows. What is not obvious is that giant yellow poplars no longer grow along the streams as they did before the loggers came through. Yet 150-foot-tall yellow poplars with trunks 7 feet in diameter may return if given the chance and several hundred more years to grow.

Clemons and Coles Forks embody nature's resilience and ability to recover. Most of the species of stream dwellers that lived in Robinson Forest before 1880 are there again today, despite splash dams, massive deforestation, erosion, fire, drought, and flash floods. Even the American beaver, missing from Buckhorn Creek since 1905, has returned on its own after a failed reintroduction effort in 1947. Unexpectedly, in 2001, flimsy stick dams appeared along Buckhorn Creek less than a mile downstream from Robinson Forest. Small streamside trees bearing the marks of beaver teeth began to appear as well. Stumps three to five inches in diameter that look like giant sharpened pencils protrude from the stream bank. Whether the big aquatic rodents will become reestablished in the forest after an absence of one hundred years is anyone's guess. What their return says, though, is that given enough time, the streams of Robinson Forest can experience ecological recovery as extirpated species slowly return on their own accord.

The streams are not resilient enough to recover from everything humans are capable of inflicting on them. All across the Cumberland Plateau, outcrops, ridgetops, and trees are being shoved down slopes to expose and mine seams of coal. Mountaintop removal has nearly leveled the Cumberland Plateau, which looks much as it did 300 million years ago, before the forces of erosion carved out the hollows. No one can really say how long it will take for a flat, reclaimed surface mine to once again become a maze of deep, V-shaped hollows, steep slopes, and narrow twisting ridgetops. I have heard some people speculate that it may take 50,000 years for outcrops to become exposed and once again loom over young hollows. Others suggest that it will require many millions of years. I suspect it will take even more time than that. The dissected plateau that existed before the practice of mountaintop removal was the result of 300 million years of erosion. Another 300 million years may well be required for nature to repair the damage. What we do know is that once it is gone, there will never be another Kentucky arrow darter.

CHAPTER 7

The Embattled Wilderness

Erik Reece

On a sunny day last November, I took a long walk up Clemons Fork to see the forest's last great display before it settled into winter dormancy. The maples and beeches that grow along the banks wore a final shimmer of orange and gold; closer to the stream, hornbeams slowly let fall their slender red leaves. A belted kingfisher swooped back and forth over the water as if running cable for an invisible suspension bridge. After a few days of rain, the current was running strong beneath the low-hanging fronds of hemlock, and at least in my mind, the pull of gravity felt even stronger than usual in the narrow catchments.

After about an hour of walking I wandered down a deer path that led through a boggy stretch of native cane. A few pale asters were still blooming in places the deer hadn't trampled. A large slab of sandstone had lodged itself in the shade of some hemlocks. It looked like a rough-hewn headstone, and I thought, not for the first time, that a woodland cove in Robinson Forest would make a satisfying final resting place. Such autumnal thoughts led me into a small clearing, and it was there, standing in the sun, that I felt a shadow pass over me. Looking up, I saw a great blue heron, its wings fully extended, glide over the clearing and come to rest on the branch of a fallen tree that stretched across a small tributary almost completely hidden by the tall grass.

The heron and I stared at one another. I felt sure I was the only human in the forest that day, and for all I know, it was the only heron. Perhaps that singularity kept our gazes fixed for almost a minute. Then *Ardea herodias*, contemporary descendant of the dinosaurs, flexed its long wings and climbed back into the air. I walked over and sat down next to the stream where the heron had lighted. I listened to the moving water for a long time, so long, in fact, that I heard it, just for a moment, take on the sound of a human voice. Then it quickly reverted back to its own native language. Which reminded me of something a friend once said when we were sitting by another stream in Robinson Forest years ago.

When I was a child, my parents used to pack my sister and me into the family station wagon and drive east to visit my great-grandmother in Hazard, Kentucky. I remember passing the small green Robinson Forest signs as we drove along Route 15 through Breathitt County. I even remember locating the forest's tiny splotch of color on my father's Rand-McNally map. But it wasn't until years later, in search of pastoral inspiration for my UK writing students (and for myself), that I actually set foot in Robinson Forest.

I drove down with a UK forestry professor I had recently met, a conservation biologist named Dave Maehr. Dave walked with me up to the fire tower and along various tributaries of Clemons Fork. As a scientist enamored with the writing of Aldo Leopold, Paul Shepard, and E. O. Wilson, Dave seemed intrigued by the prospect of actually bringing writing students into Robinson Forest and perhaps sparking a mutually productive conversation between the sciences and the humanities. Dave's area of study was large mammals, or "charismatic megafauna," of which he was himself a pretty demonstrative example. Dave was brash and voluble and, as I learned later, the country's leading expert on the Florida panther. As we sat on a fallen tree stump and listened to the thrumming of ruffed grouse, he expressed his outrage that UK's president and board of trustees would even entertain the thought of logging or mining Robinson Forest. Destroying the rich genetic information contained within Robinson Forest would be equivalent, he said, to Julius Caesar's burning of the library at Alexandria in 48 BCE.

"Nobody on the board of trustees would recommend burning books in the UK libraries to heat campus buildings," Dave said, poking at the leaf litter with a dead stick. "That would be insane." Yet, mining Robinson Forest for coal and money would be exactly the same kind of destruction of invaluable knowledge. "Because we can't put a dollar value on these kinds of assets," Dave said, "they get ignored or relegated to some secondary status."

And that fact has always made it difficult to argue for the value of an eastern Kentucky ecosystem against the value of a short ton of eastern Kentucky coal. You can ship the coal up the Kentucky River, after all, and quickly cash a paycheck. The "payoff" of an intact Robinson Forest is less obvious because it cannot quickly be converted into dollars and its value can be measured only by future generations of students and researchers. A strip mine, on the other hand, has no future. Once the coal is gone, it is a dead zone. And once the profits from that coal are spent, any nostalgia or remorse is meaningless and devoid of value.

As Dave spoke, he punctuated his comments by pointing skyward and naming the songbirds calling in the distance: Carolina wren, ovenbird, black-and-white warbler. He said he also had no patience for the idea that had been circulating around the forestry department that Robinson Forest should pay for its maintenance and management through logging 85 percent of its watersheds over a seventy-year rotation. Instead, Dave imagined establishing a value-added, regional wood products industry that would use Robinson Forest timber harvested in a sustainable fashion. After all, UK already manages a large wood shop, called the Wood Center, twenty miles up the road at its Quicksand station. In the spirit of E. O. Robinson's charge that the forest be used to better the lives of eastern Kentuckians, that Wood Center could incubate such an enterprise. Dave's idea was a "Robinson Forest" line of wood products that would benefit a local artisan economy and could be marketed in larger Kentucky cities as sustainably produced tables, chairs, and cabinets. The bottom line, he said, was this: any research and resource management activities that take place in Robinson Forest should enhance the development of Robinson Forest as the region's most unique ecosystem, not diminish them.

"Have you ever just sat here and listened, I mean really *listened* to the forest?" Dave asked. I shook my head no. "Listen to the wind, the water, the birdsong. What are they saying?" We pondered that question in silence for a few minutes. Then Dave grinned and said, "Don't you think that would make for a good writing assignment?"

I agreed that it would, and so it has proven to be in the years since. The assignment I give my students is to consider not only what humans need from the land, but what kind of husbandry and stewardship the land needs from us. Such thinking tends to breed humility, which I now think is what Dave was really calling for.

After that initial visit, I took a number of trips to Robinson Forest with Dave, his graduate students, and my own undergraduates. Dave and I talked a great deal about how the forest should best be managed, speculated on courses we might teach together in the future, and became good friends. Then one Sunday morning in June 2008, I picked up the Lexington paper to read that Dave was dead.

He had been in Florida conducting an aerial survey of black bears when his single-engine plane stalled, then nose-dived into the ground, killing Dave and his pilot instantly. As is often the case with a sudden death, I couldn't quite register what I was reading. There was a photograph of Dave in the paper; he was holding a bear cub. The longer I stared at it, the more unreal it seemed. I couldn't square the fact of Dave's absence with my subjective reality that still included his presence in the world. And it took awhile to reach the point where Dave's absence eventually led to the realization that the rest of us—his family, friends, students, and colleagues—had to move forward.

Some time after Dave's memorial service, I dug up a letter he had written to his colleagues in the UK forestry department a few months before he died. In it he expressed alarm that potential logging and mining in Robinson Forest would jeopardize eight decades of stewardship by the university. He wrote: "I have maintained since the day I first heard of Robinson Forest that its primary value was as an exemplar of mature mixed mesophytic forests with characteristics of the wilderness that greeted Daniel Boone and the long riflemen." Dave argued that the best combination of research, teaching, and education would include activities that take advantage of and enhance "the continuing development of the old-growth characteristics that with each passing year make Robinson Forest incrementally more unique and valuable to the

University of Kentucky, the people of eastern Kentucky, and the world."
I think Dave was right: that is exactly the kind of research that must go
forward in Robinson Forest if it is to maintain its integrity, stability, and
beauty, and if it is to have a future that enhances the reputation of the
university, the opportunities of its students, and the streams and rivers
that flow away from its headwaters.

Now that the world has reached, and passed, what James Hansen,
the country's leading climatologist, calls the tipping point of climate
change—350 parts per million of CO_2 in the atmosphere—we are about
to enter this country's most important era of forestry. Currently forests
absorb more than a quarter of the world's carbon dioxide—the output
from all of our cars and trucks. Yet far more research remains to be
done if we are to understand both the effects climate change will have
on forests and the role forests might play in mitigating its potentially
catastrophic effects. Right now, excess carbon in the atmosphere is killing forests worldwide, and we are only beginning to understand forests'
potential for capturing that carbon. What is more, the forests of the eastern United States are among the most important "carbon sinks" in our
hemisphere.

Researchers at a three-thousand-acre forest owned and managed by
Harvard University are measuring carbon flux: the rate at which the
forest absorbs and releases carbon. The *New York Times* recently called
Harvard Forest "one of the world's most intensively studied patches of
woods." The same should be said of Robinson Forest. Yet, UK forestry
professor Thomas Barnes wrote recently in *Kentucky Woodlands Magazine*
that "Kentucky lags far behind other states with respect to conducting
research on the present and future implications of climate change." Given
that Robinson Forest is four times the size of Harvard's research forest,
even more significant climate research could be done here. That research
would tell us a great deal about how the mountain ecosystems of central
and southern Appalachia are responding, or might respond, to the world's
rapidly changing climate. Levels of carbon dioxide in the atmosphere
have risen 40 percent since the start of the Industrial Revolution. Given
that central Appalachia has made a substantial contribution to that figure

in the form of burning bituminous coal, there would be a certain kind of justice, an elegant recompense, if the research that came out of Robinson Forest helped ameliorate the damage of the last one hundred years.

Such research would certainly have economic value, but it would also have ethical value, ecological value, and spiritual value. And if, as a region, our collective conscience began to change because of that knowledge, then the dollar value of something would cease to be our only standard of worth. We would stop burning the future by converting it into money. We would invent a far more attractive and enduring vision of the future, and we would have a better system of values to guide us there.

Robinson Forest is many things: it is one of the most important ecosystems in Appalachia, it is a laboratory for crucial research and teaching, and it is a gift held in trust for future generations of Kentuckians. But it is also a *model* for how we must proceed in our habitation of the natural world. In fact, Robinson Forest represents a model for an entirely new definition of "economy," whereby our American systems of exchange, both of wealth and energy, are brought in line with the most important and inescapable economy of nature. It is a lesson in home economics. The words "ecology" and "economy" both derive from the Greek root *oikos*, which refers to the daily operation of a household. What we as twenty-first-century Americans must finally come to understand is that the economy of consumption operates in direct opposition to, and at the peril of, the economy of nature. At the Land Institute in Salina, Kansas, Wes Jackson is proving that a perennial crop agriculture that follows the natural laws of the prairie will eliminate the great problems of modern agriculture: erosion, pesticide use, loss of biodiversity, and greenhouse gas emissions. Just as Jackson took his lessons for a new agricultural economy from the prairie, we in Kentucky should look to Robinson Forest as a model for a sustainable, post-coal economy. We must replace the industrial logic of the strip mine with the much more ancient wisdom of the forest.

A watershed is, by its very nature, self-sufficient, symbiotic, conservative, decentralized, and diverse. It circulates its own wealth over and over. It generates no waste and does not "externalize" the cost of "production" onto other watersheds, other streams, and other valleys. In a watershed, *all* energy is renewable and all resource use is sustainable. In this sense, the watershed economy is the exact opposite of a strip mine. It purifies air and water, holds soil in place, enriches humus, and sequesters carbon. That is to say, a watershed economy *improves* the land and thus improves the lives of the people who inhabit that particular place. It is an economy based not on the unsustainable, short-sighted logic of never-ending *growth*, which robs the future to meet the overinflated needs of the present, but rather on maintaining the health, well-being, and stability of the human and the land communities.

Certainly Henry David Thoreau was thinking about such things when he wrote in 1862, "In wilderness is the preservation of the world." One hundred and fifty years later, biologists and climatologists are showing that he was more right than he could have known. To abandon wilderness places like Robinson Forest would be to abandon ourselves. To ignore the natural laws of its watersheds for the logic of our own industrial imagination would be to abandon our better selves—to abandon a sustainable future for the sake of short-term avarice and indulgence. But to preserve the world will mean learning the lessons of Robinson Forest, and in doing so learning to preserve that embattled wilderness.

Works Cited and Consulted

Delcourt, Paul A., Hazel R. Delcourt, Cecil R. Ison, William E. Sharp, and Kristen J. Gremillion. "Prehistoric Human Use of Fire, the Eastern Agricultural Complex, and Appalachian Oak-Chestnut Forests: Paleoecology of Cliff Place Pond, Kentucky." *American Antiquity* 63 (1998): 263–78.

Freinkel, Susan. *American Chestnut: The Life, Death, and Rebirth of a Perfect Tree.* Berkeley: University of California Press, 2007.

Gillis, Justin. "With Deaths of Forests, a Loss of Key Climate Protectors." *New York Times*, October 1, 2001, sec. A.

Goodell, Jeff. *Big Coal.* New York: Mariner, 2007.

Harris, Ann G., E. Tuttle, and Sherwood D. Tuttle. *Geology of National Parks.* 5th ed. Dubuque, Iowa: Kendall/Hunt, 1997.

Jaffe, Eric. "This Side of Paradise: Discovering Why the Human Mind Needs Nature." *APS Observer* 23, no. 5 (May–June 2010).

Krupa, James J. "Night Chorus." *Nebraskaland*, April 1991.

Krupa, James J., and Michael J. Lacki. *Mammals of Robinson Forest: Species Composition of an Isolated, Mixed-Mesophytic Forest on the Cumberland Plateau in Southeastern Kentucky.* Museum of Texas Tech University Special Publications 45 (2002).

Krupa, James J., and Andrew Sih. "Fishing Spiders, Green Sunfish, and a Stream-Dwelling Water Strider: Male-Female Conflict and Prey Responses to Single versus Multiple Predator Environments." *Oecologia* 117 (1998): 258–65.

Leopold, Aldo. *Sand County Almanac.* London: Oxford University Press, 1968.

Loewenstein, Edward F. "Silviculture and the Long-Term Dynamics of Single-Tree Selection of Pioneer Forest." In *Pioneer Forest*, ed. James M. Guldin, Greg F. Iffrig, and Susan L. Flader. Asheville, N.C.: Southern Research Station, 2008.

Lucke, Jamie. "UK Enters New Era for Robinson Forest." *Lexington Herald-Leader*, March 24, 1991, sec. B.

———. "UK Environmentalists Halt Fight against Mining near Robinson Forest." *Lexington Herald-Leader*, March 19, 1991, sec. A.

Maehr, David. Letter. Typescript. September 19, 2007.

McBride, Kim A. "Historical Cultural Resources of the Project Area." In *Archeological Site Distributions on the Cumberland Plateau of Eastern Kentucky*. Lexington, Ky.: U.S. Department of the Interior, 1990.

McCarthy, Cormac. *The Road*. New York: Knopf, 2006.

Miller, Jim Wayne. *The Brier Poems*. Frankfort, Ky.: Gnomon Press, 1997.

Muir, John. *A Thousand-Mile Walk to the Gulf.* Boston and New York: Houghton Mifflin, 1916.

Nesbitt, Roger. "UK, Coal Company Negotiating to Prevent Mining in Robinson Forest." *Lexington Herald-Leader*, August 5, 1987, sec. A.

Oliver, Mary. *New and Selected Poems*. Vol. 2. Boston: Beacon Press, 2005.

Overstreet, John C. *Robinson Forest Inventory 1980–1982*. Lexington, Ky.: University of Kentucky Department of Forestry, 1984.

Pond, Greg. "Effects of Surface Mining and Residential Land Use on Headwater Stream Biotic Integrity in the Eastern Kentucky Coalfield Region." Kentucky Department for Environmental Protection and the Division of Water, 2004.

Robinson, Gordon. *The Forest and the Trees*. Washington, D.C.: Island Press, 1988.

Rouse, Shelly. "Troubles on Troublesome." Kentucky Historical Society.

Slone, Verna Mae. *What My Heart Wants to Tell*. Washington: New Republic Books, 1979.

Still, James. *River of Earth*. New York: Popular Library, 1940.

———. *The Wolfpen Poems*. Berea, Ky.: Berea College Press, 1986.

Sussenbach, Tom. *Archeological Site Distributions*. Lexington, Ky.: U.S. Department of the Interior, 1990.

Urch, Kakie. "Robinson Forest Group Resurfaces." *Lexington Herald-Leader*, February 20, 1990, sec. B.

Whitehead, Alfred North. *Science and the Modern World*. New York: New American Library, 1959.

Wirzba, Norman. *The Paradise of God*. Oxford: Oxford University Press, 2003.